LITTLE
ACORN
BOOKS

USING
CRAYONS,
SCISSORS & GLUE
LITTLE PROJECTS FOR LITTLE HANDS

by Marilynn G. Barr

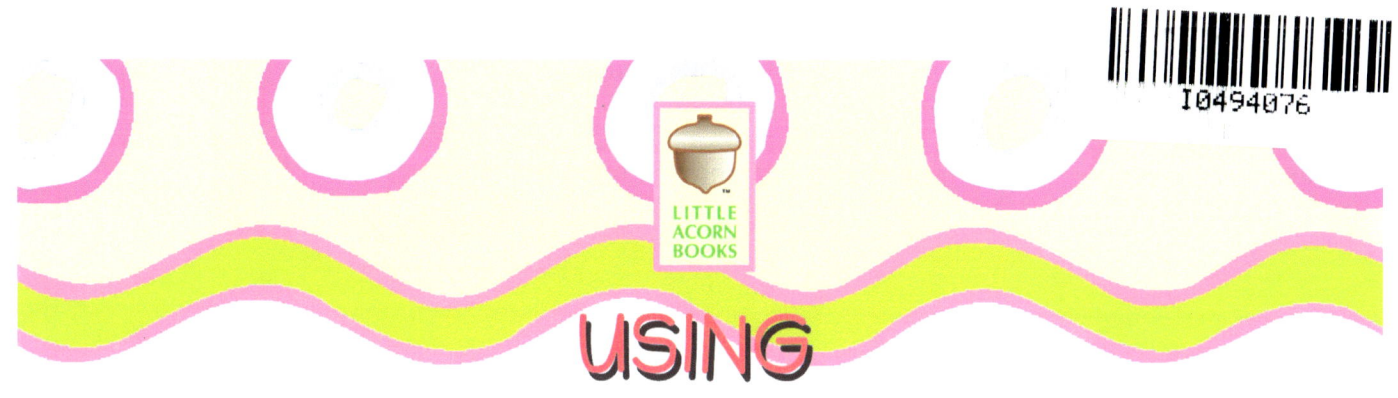

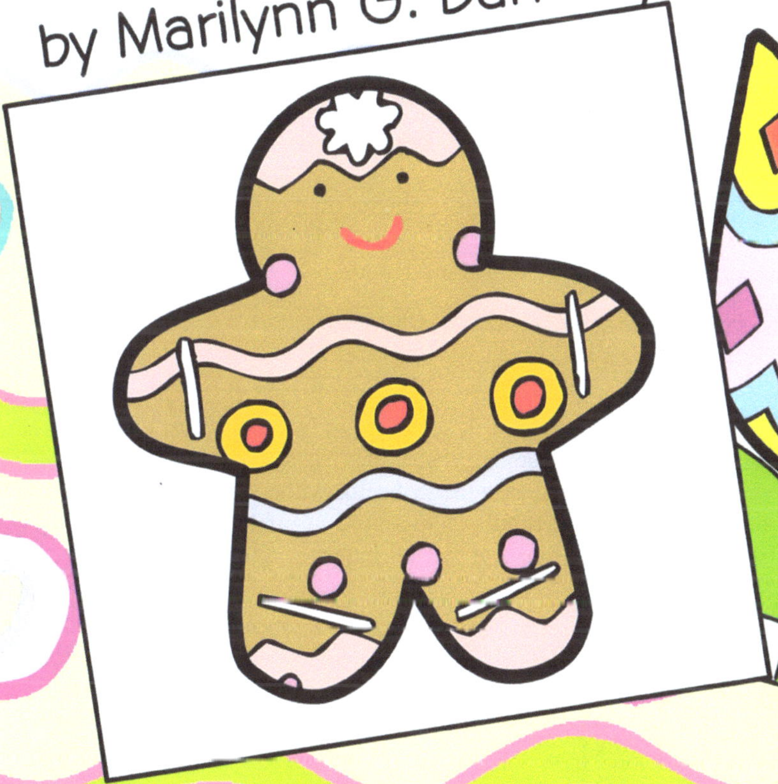

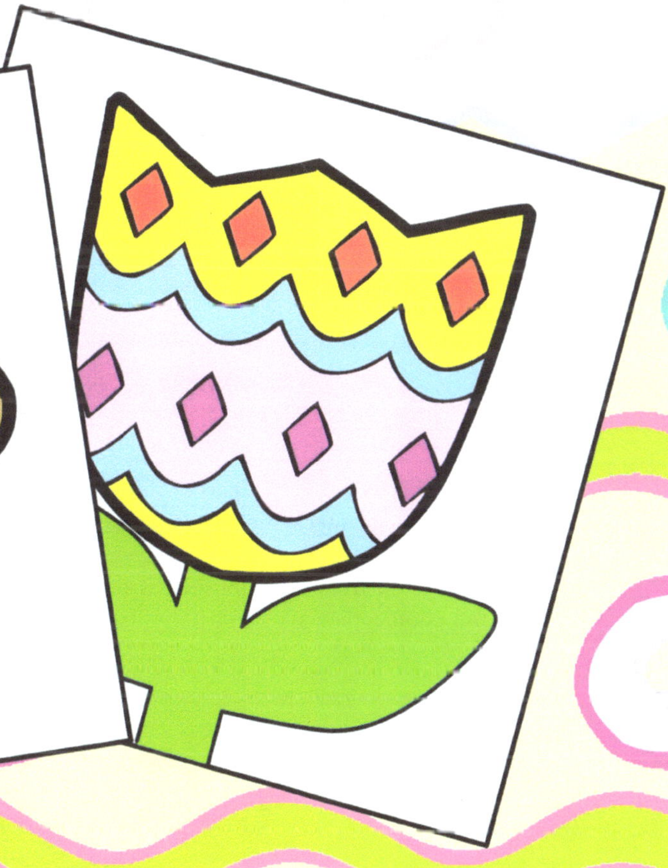

Contents

LAB20043
USING CRAYONS, SCISSORS & GLUE for CRAFTS
©2010, Little Acorn Books

Published

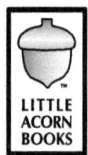

LITTLE
ACORN
BOOKS

by Little Acorn Books, a division of Little Acorn & Associates, Inc.
Post Office Box 8787
Greensboro, NC 27419-0787

ISBN 978-0-9844010-0-0

Printed in the United States of America
0 9 8 7 6 5 4 3 2 1

USING CRAYONS, SCISSORS & GLUE for CRAFTS
Little Projects for Little Hands

MATERIALS:

crayons
scissors
glue
paint brush
glitter
pom poms (assorted sizes)
buttons (assorted sizes)
yarn
cotton balls
cereal Os
dried beans
ribbon
construction paper
hole punch

Repetition is key in developing early skills. Using Crayons, Scissors, & Glue for Crafts features 32 projects designed to reinforce tracing, coloring, cutting and pasting skills . as well as following directions in a repeating format. Projects range from easy to challenging and offer little hands plenty of motor skills practice.

Each project features a *Give a Helping Hand* logo Give a helping hand. alert for adult helpers. Beginning as well as advanced learners may require some assistance completing a project.

Scissor icons identify the cards and patterns to cut out along bold lines each project page.

FRAMING A LITTLE PROJECT:

1. Measure and cut construction paper slightly larger than a project card.
2. Glue the finished project card in the center of the construction paper cutout.

A LITTLE PROJECT ORNAMENT:

1. Measure and cut construction paper slightly larger than a project card.
2. Glue the finished project card in the center of the construction paper cutout.
3. Punch two holes along the top of the construction paper frame.
4. Measure, cut, lace, and tie a length of yarn through the holes for hanging.

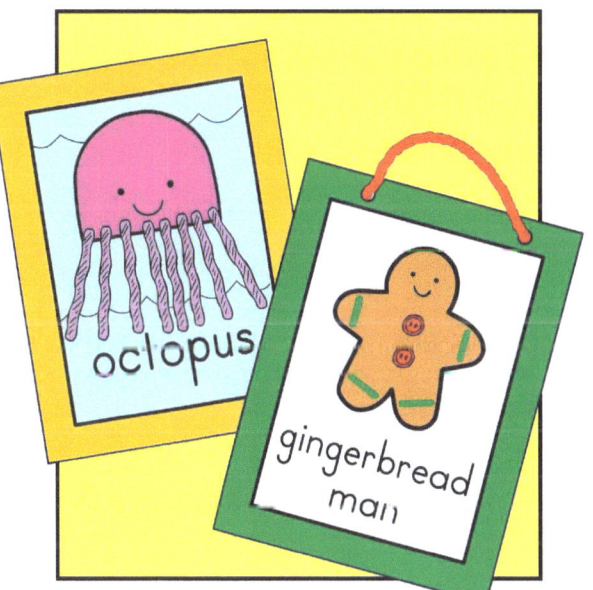

A CUTTING PRACTICE COLLAGE:

Create a collage with cutting practice shapes and poster board. Color and glue cutting practice strips and shapes on a sheet of poster board. Write each contributor's name on the collage. Display the finished collage.

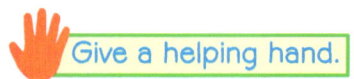
A Little Turtle Project

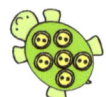 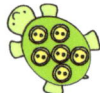

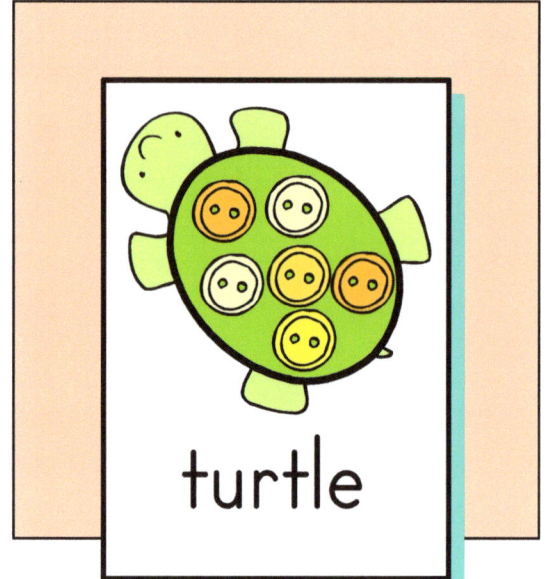

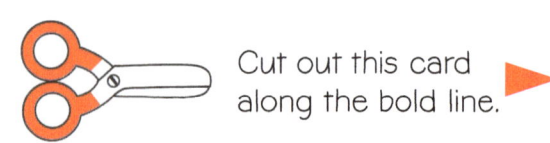

turtle

turtle

Cut out this card along the bold line. ▶

Cut out this pattern along the bold line. ▼

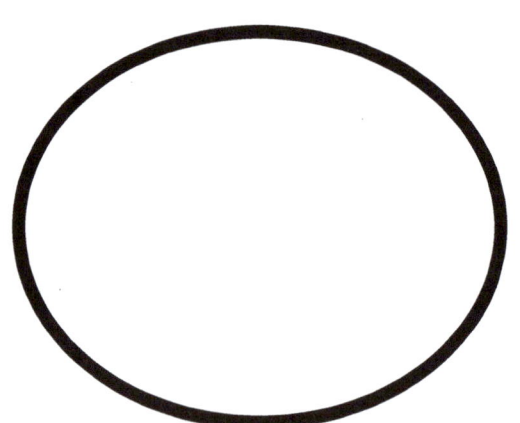

What You Will Need:

crayons   scissors
glue   buttons

What to Do:

1. Trace the dotted line.
2. Color and cut out the card.
3. Color and cut out the turtle shell pattern.
4. Glue the turtle shell cutout on the card.
5. Glue buttons on the turtle shell.

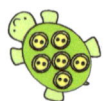 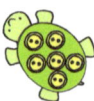 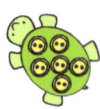 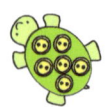 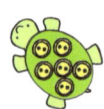 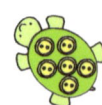 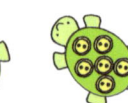 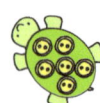 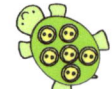

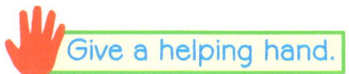

Give a helping hand.

A Little Egg Project

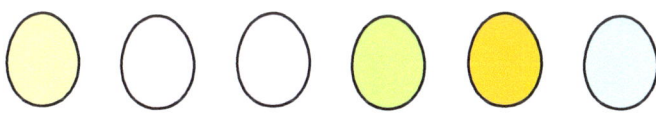

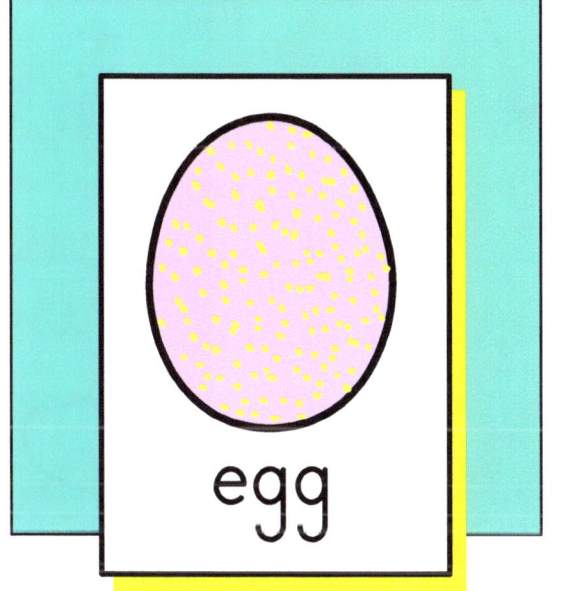

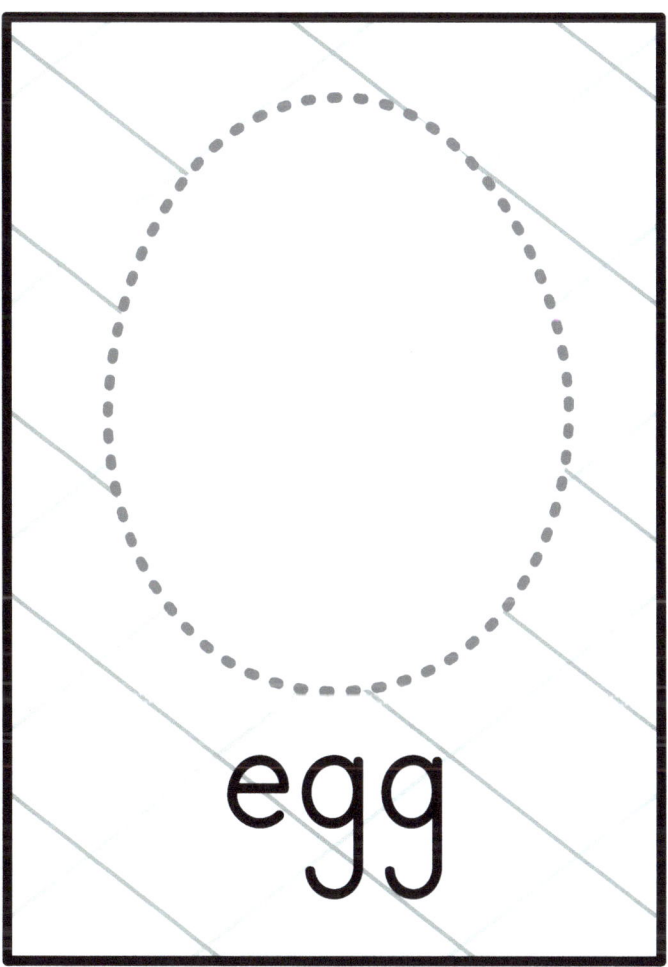

egg

Cut out this card along the bold line. ▶

Cut out this pattern along the bold line. ▼

What You Will Need:
crayons   scissors
paint brush   glue
glitter

What to Do:
1. Trace the dotted line.
2. Color and cut out the card.
3. Color the egg pattern.
4. Color, cut out, and glue the egg cutout on the card.
5. Apply glue with a paint brush, then sprinkle glitter on the egg.

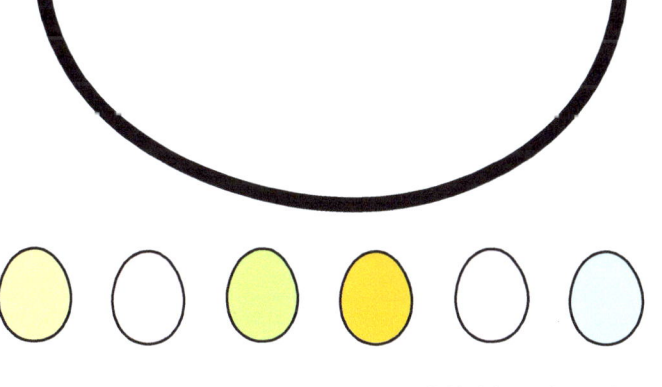

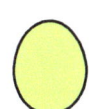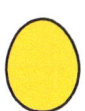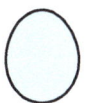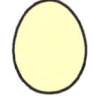

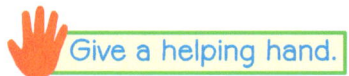

A Little Balloon Project

     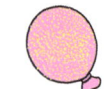 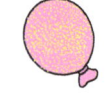

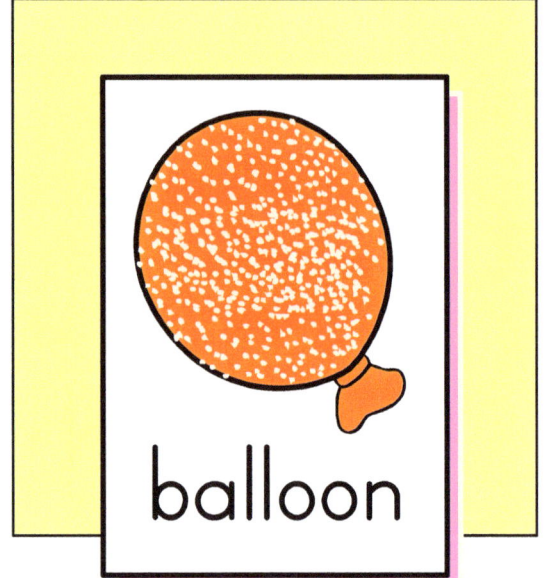

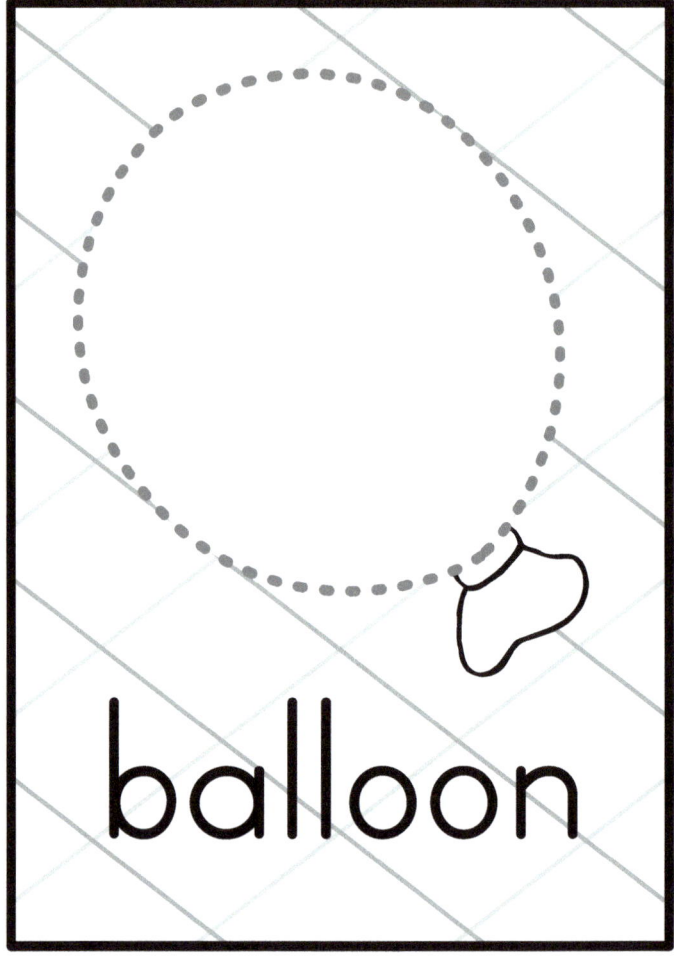

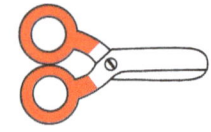 Cut out this card along the bold line. ▶

What You Will Need:

crayons	scissors
paint brush	glue
glitter	yarn

Cut out this pattern along the bold line. ▼

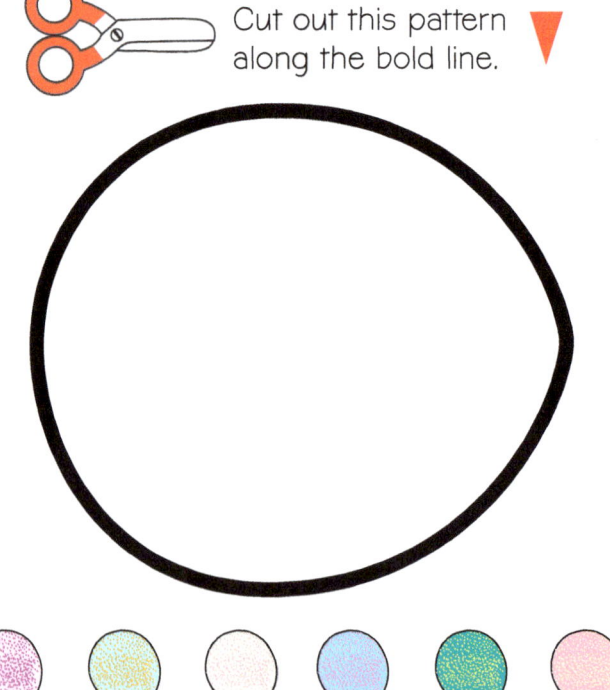

What to Do:

1. Trace the dotted line.
2. Color and cut out the card.
3. Color and cut out the balloon pattern.
4. Glue the balloon cutout on the card.
5. Apply glue with a paint brush, then sprinkle glitter on the balloon.

  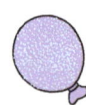 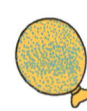 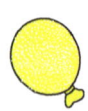 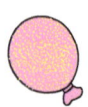 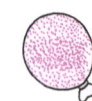   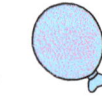 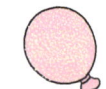

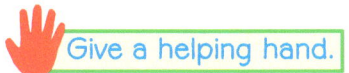 Give a helping hand.

A Little Ship Project

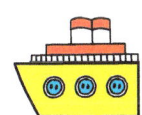 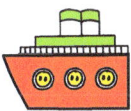 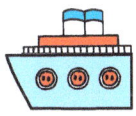 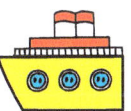

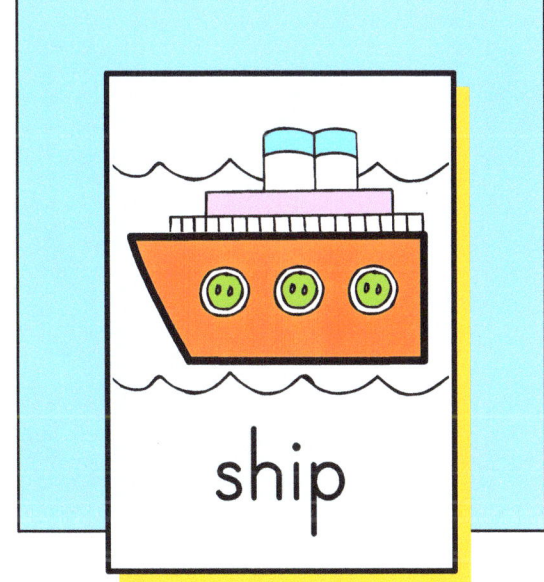

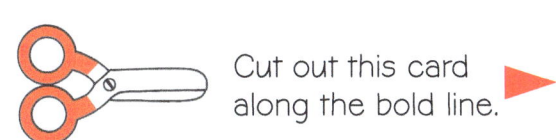 ship

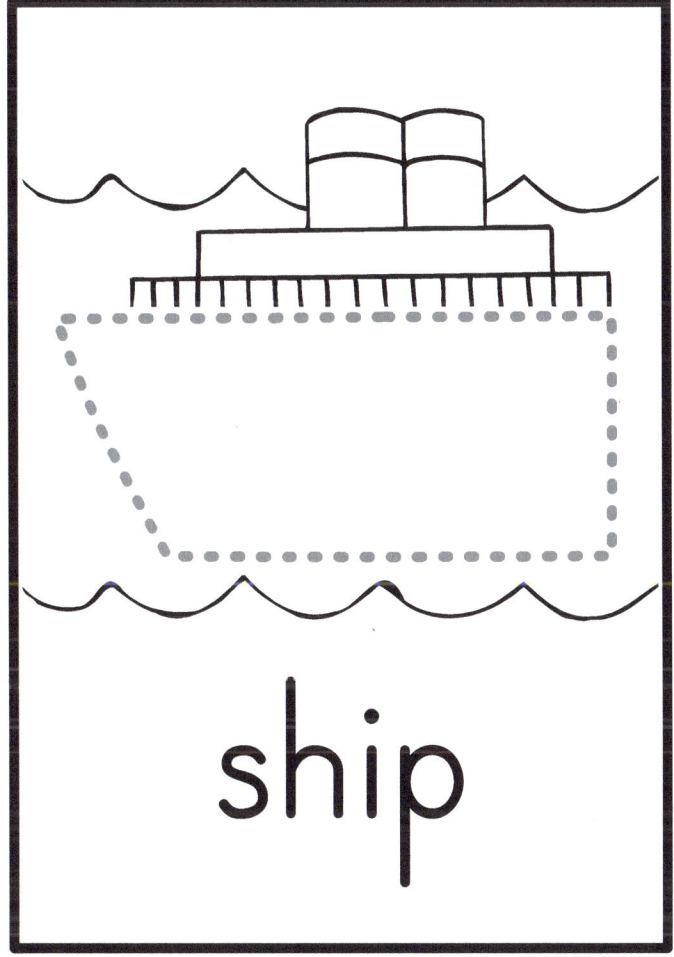

ship

Cut out this card along the bold line. ▶

Cut out this pattern along the bold line. ▼

What You Will Need:

crayons   scissors
glue   3 buttons

What to Do:

1. Trace the dotted line.
2. Color and cut out the card.
3. Color and cut out the ship pattern.
4. Glue the ship cutout on the card.
5. Glue 3 buttons on the ship.

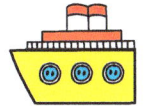 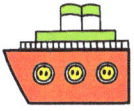 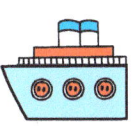 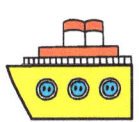 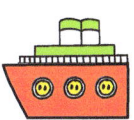 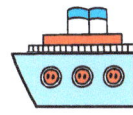 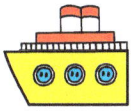  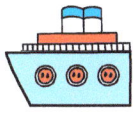

A Little Octopus Project

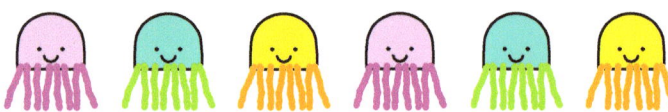

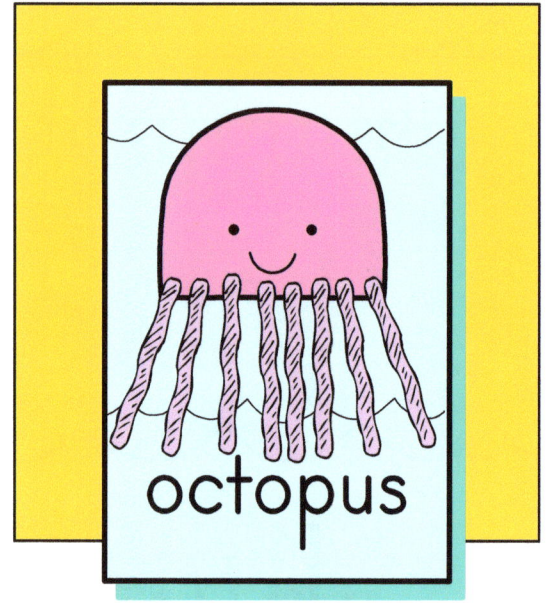

octopus

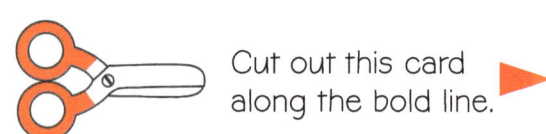
Cut out this card along the bold line. ▶

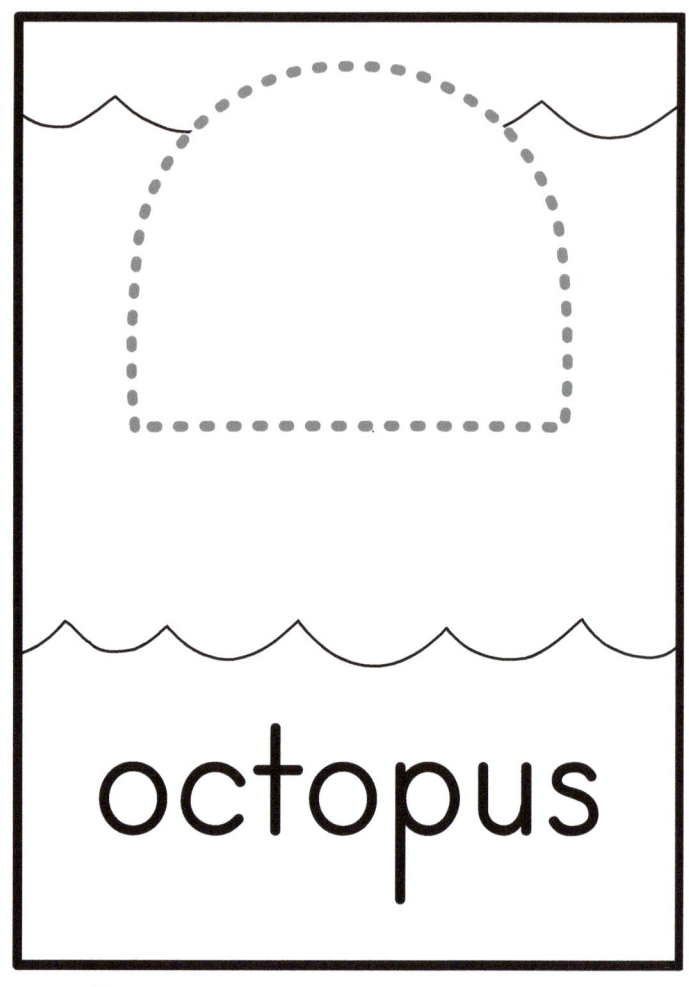

octopus

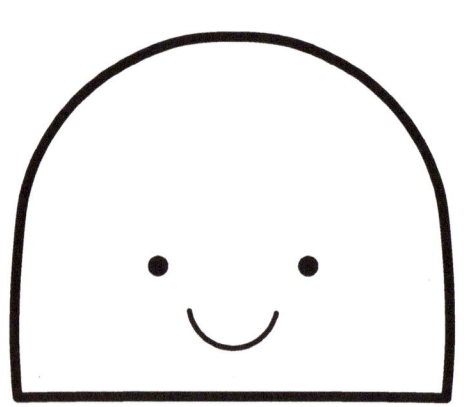
Cut out this pattern along the bold line. ▼

What You Will Need:

crayons   scissors
glue   yarn

What to Do:

1. Trace the dotted line.
2. Color and cut out the card.
3. Color and cut out the octopus pattern.
4. Glue the octopus cutout on the card.
5. Cut and glue eight yarn legs on the octopus.

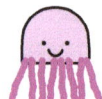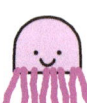

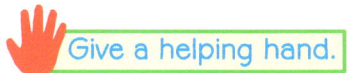 **Give a helping hand.**

A Little Ladybug Project

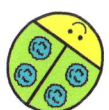 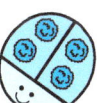 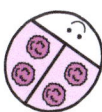 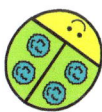 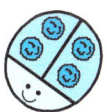

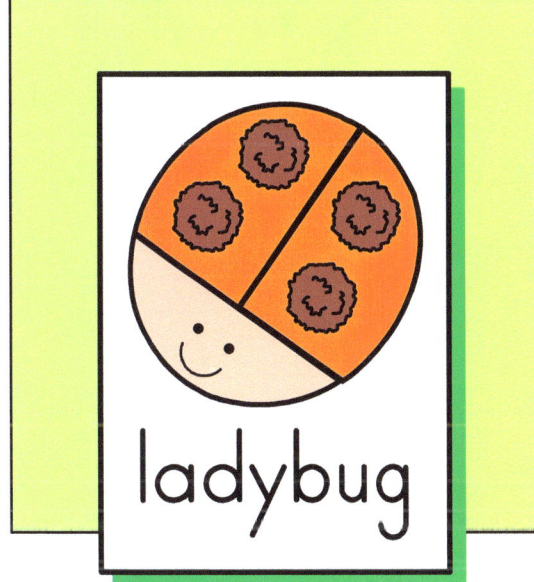

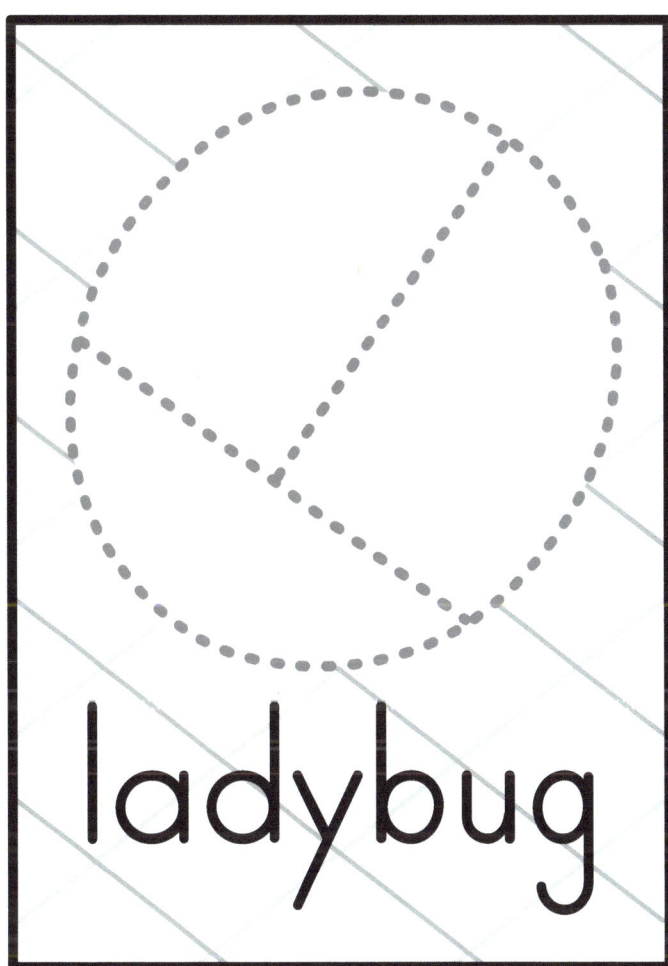

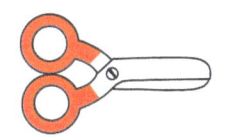 Cut out this card along the bold line. ▶

Cut out this pattern along the bold line. ▼

What You Will Need:

crayons   scissors
glue   4 pom poms

What to Do:

1. Trace the dotted lines.
2. Color and cut out the card.
3. Color and cut out the ladybug patterns.
4. Glue the ladybug cutouts on the card.
5. Glue 4 pom poms on the ladybug.

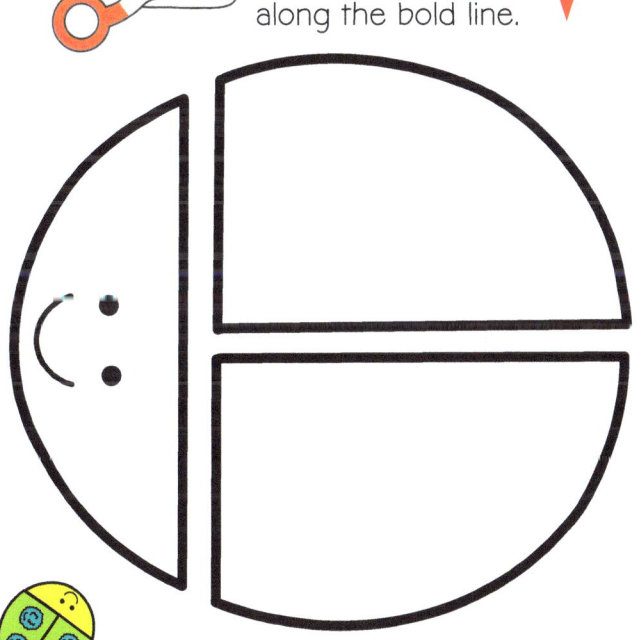

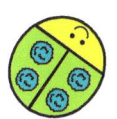 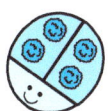 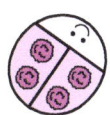 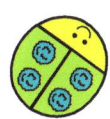 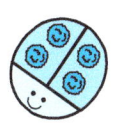 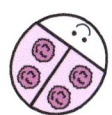 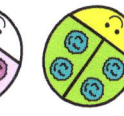

A Little Apple Project

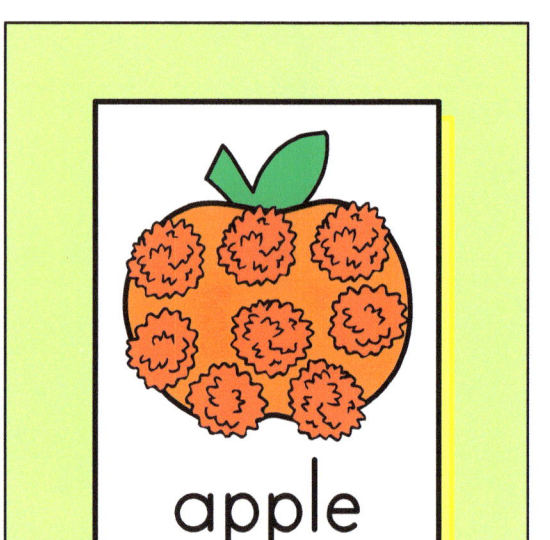

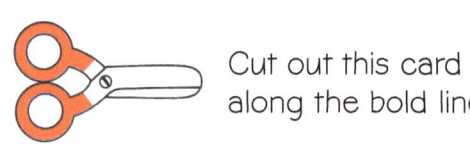
apple

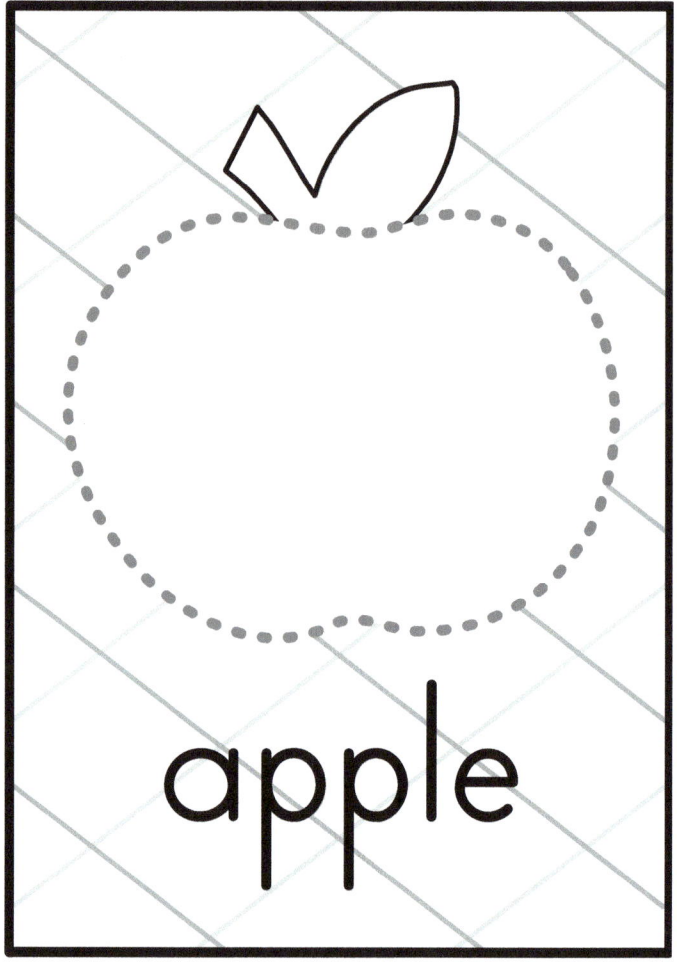

apple

Cut out this card along the bold line. ▶

Cut out this pattern along the bold line. ▼

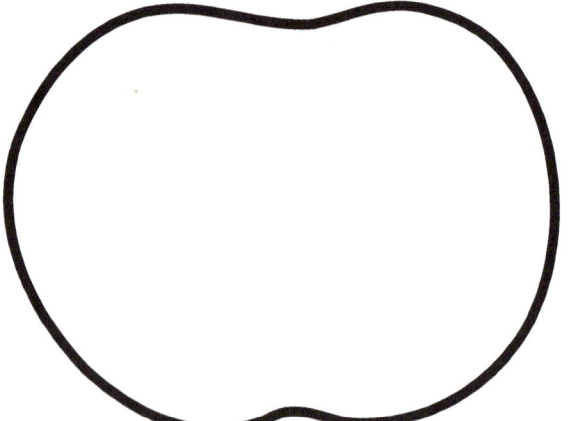

What You Will Need:

crayons   scissors
glue   red, yellow, or green pom poms

What to Do:

1. Trace the dotted line.
2. Color and cut out the card.
3. Color and cut out the apple pattern.
4. Glue the apple cutout on the card.
5. Glue pom poms on the apple.

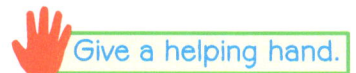 Give a helping hand.

A Little Cupcake Project

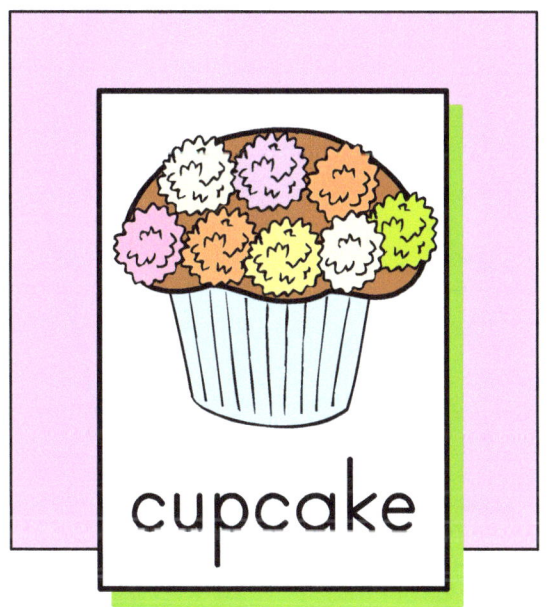

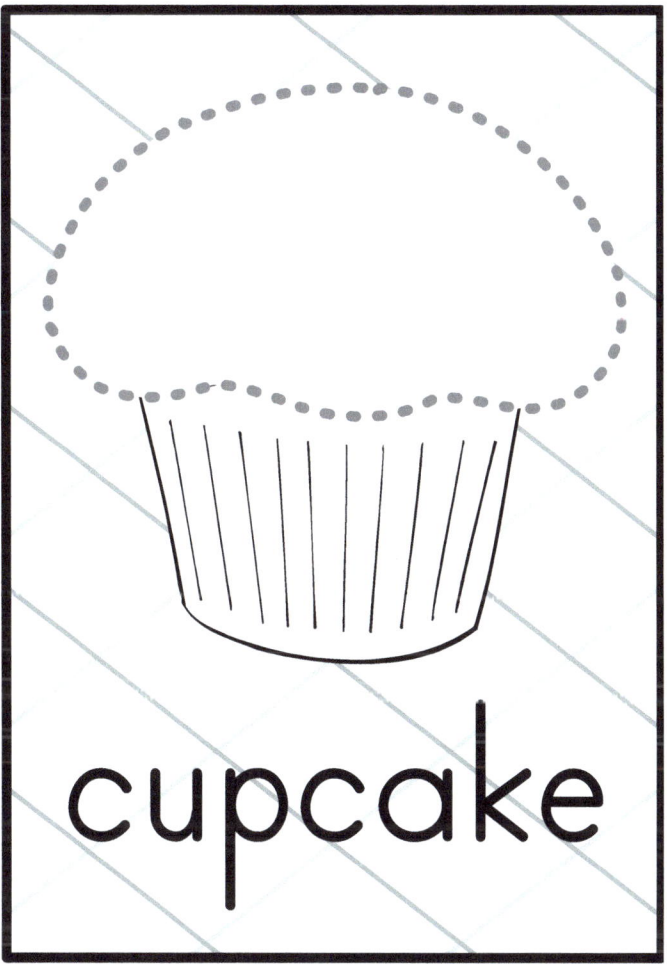

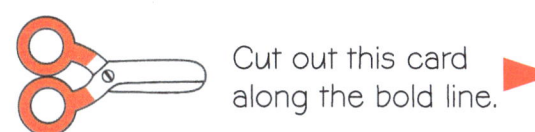 Cut out this card along the bold line. ▶

Cut out this pattern along the bold line. ▼

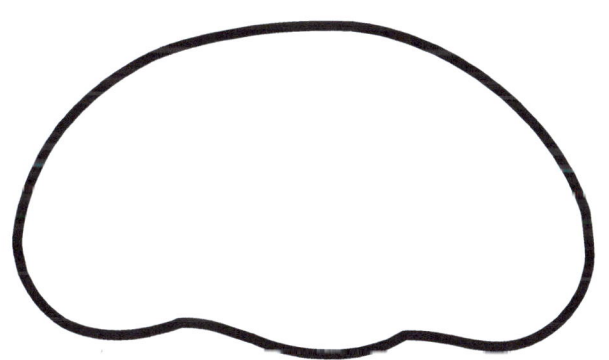

What You Will Need:

crayons   scissors
glue   pom poms

What to Do:

1. Trace the dotted line.
2. Color and cut out the card.
3. Color and cut out the cupcake pattern.
4. Glue the cupcake cutout on the card.
5. Glue pom poms on the cupcake.

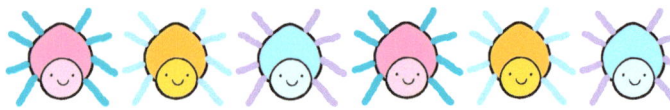
A Little Spider Project

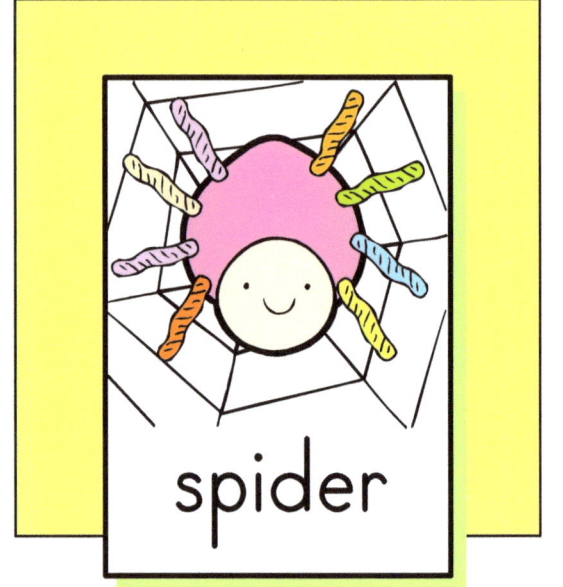

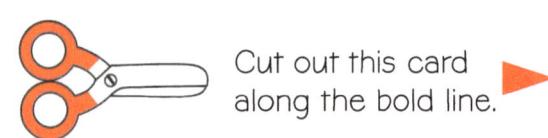

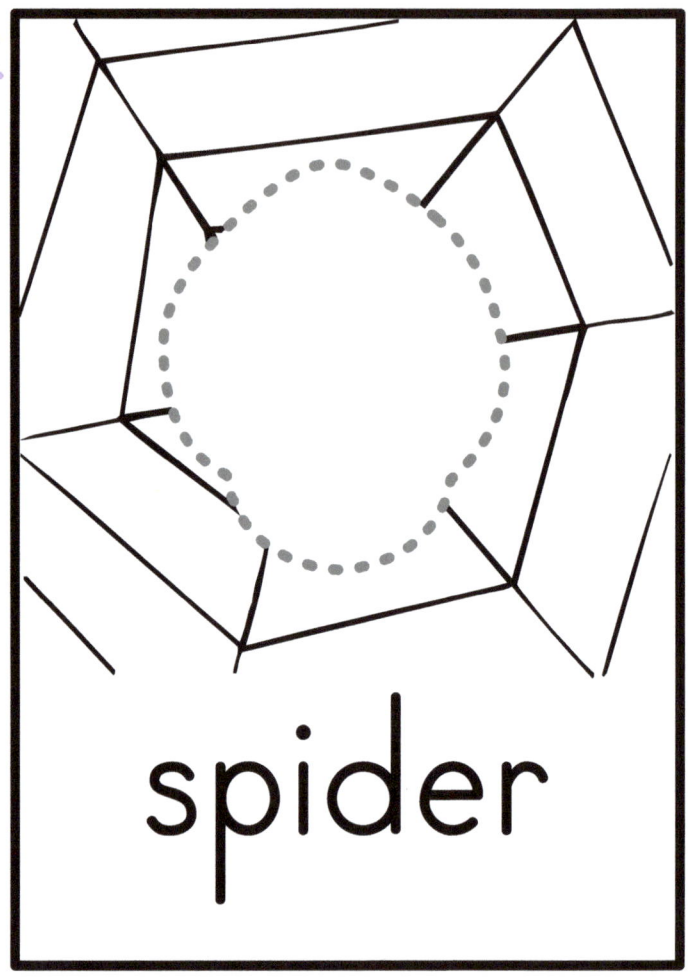

✂ Cut out this card along the bold line. ▶

✂ Cut out this pattern along the bold line. ▼

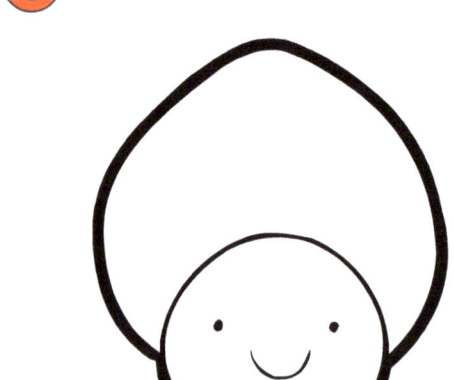

What You Will Need:

crayons   scissors
glue   yarn

What to Do:

1. Trace the dotted line.
2. Color and cut out the card.
3. Color and cut out the spider pattern.
4. Glue the spider cutout on the card.
5. Cut and glue eight yarn legs on the spider.

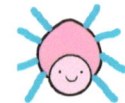   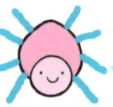  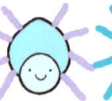 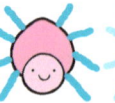   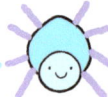

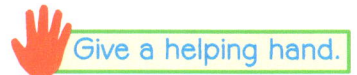 Give a helping hand.

A Little Leaf Project

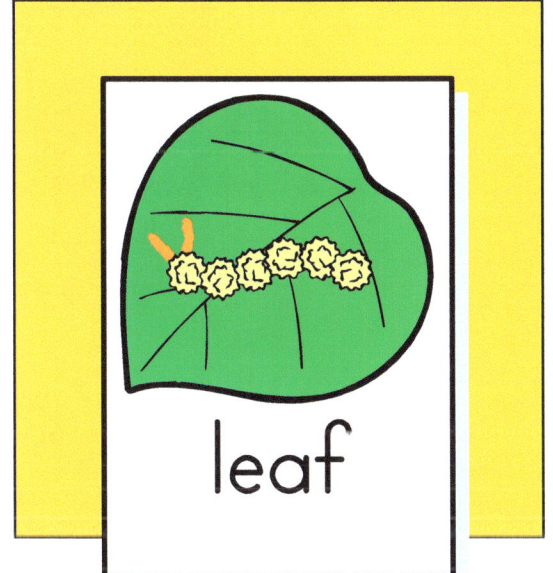

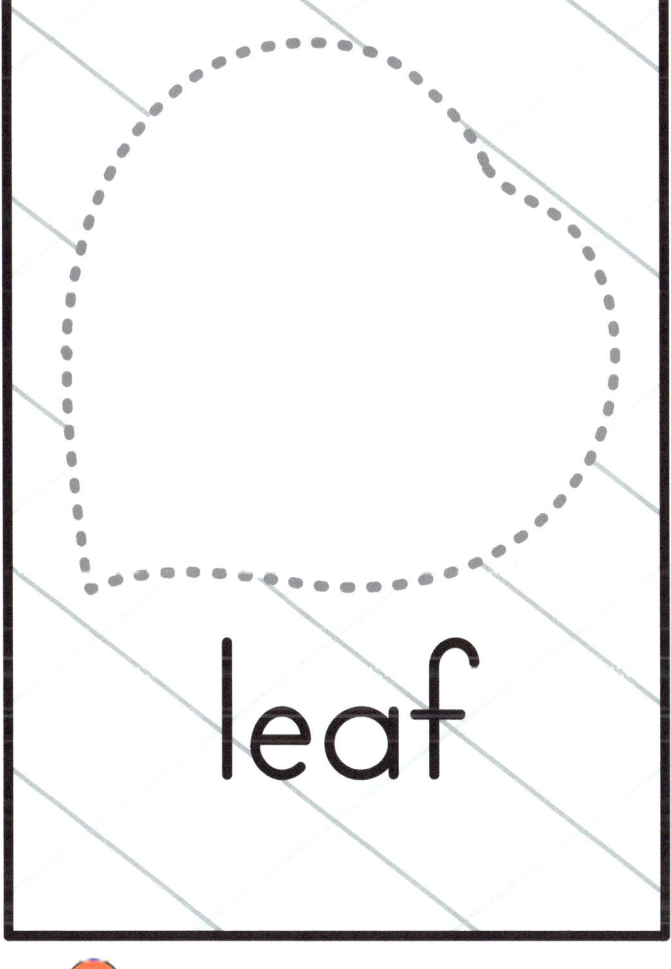

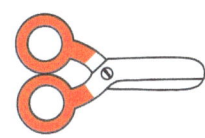 Cut out this card along the bold line. ▶

What You Will Need:

crayons   scissors
glue   6 small pom poms
pipe cleaner

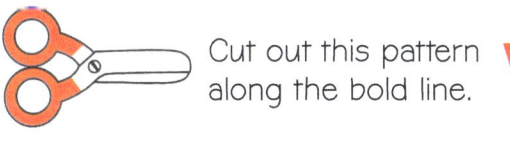 Cut out this pattern along the bold line. ▼

What to Do:

1. Trace the dotted line.
2. Color and cut out the card.
3. Color and cut out the leaf pattern.
4. Glue the leaf cutout on the card.
5. Glue 6 small pom poms on the leaf to form a caterpillar.
6. Cut and glue two pipe cleaner antennae on the caterpillar.

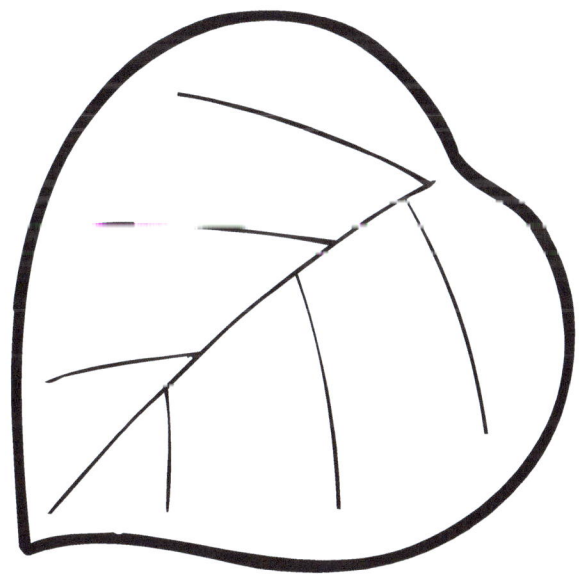

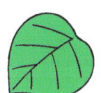 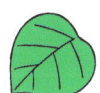 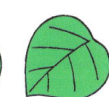 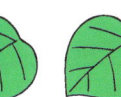 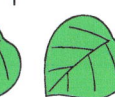 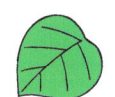 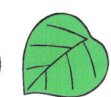

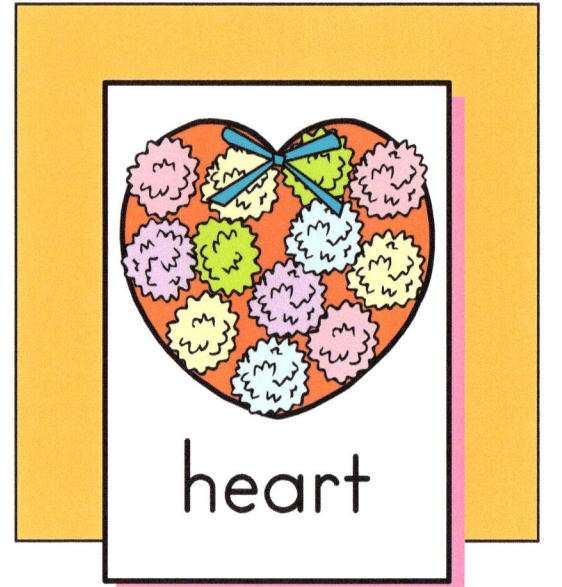

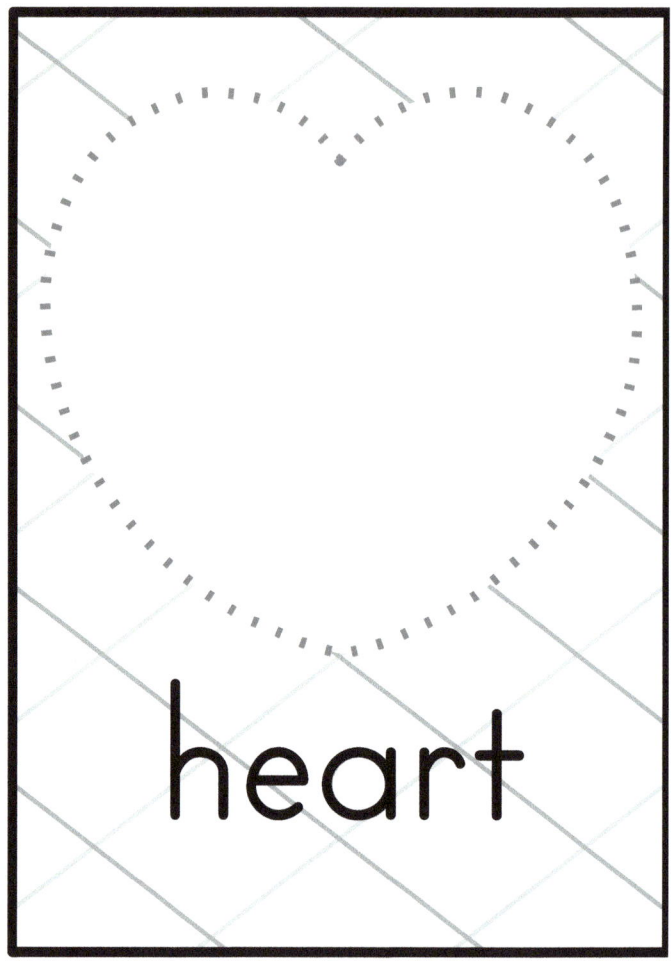

heart

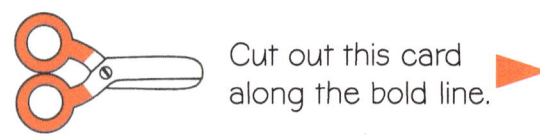
Cut out this card along the bold line.

Cut out this pattern along the bold line.

What You Will Need:

crayons   scissors
glue   pom poms
ribbon

What to Do:

1. Trace the dotted line.
2. Color and cut out the card.
3. Color and cut out the heart pattern.
4. Glue the heart cutout on the card.
5. Glue pom poms on the heart.
6. Cut, tie, and glue a ribbon bow at the top of the heart.

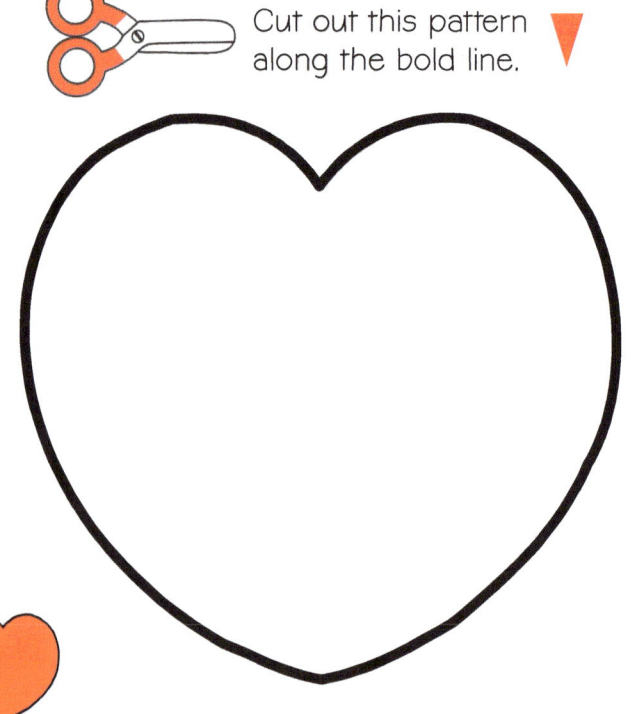

 Give a helping hand.

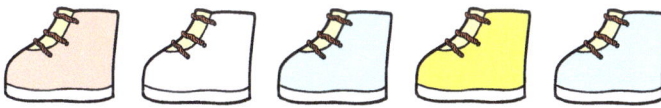

A Little Shoe Project

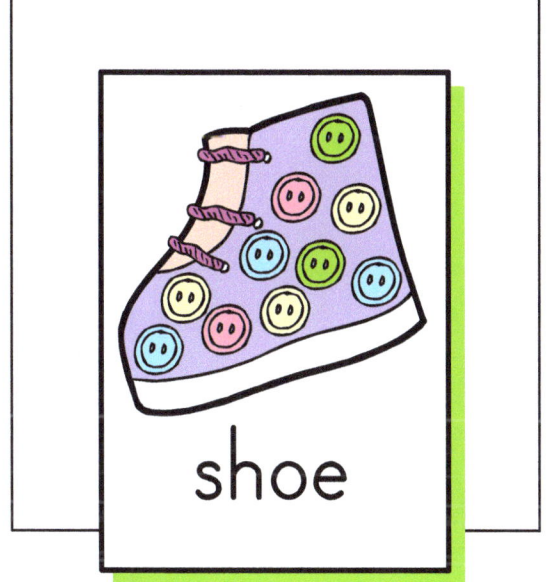

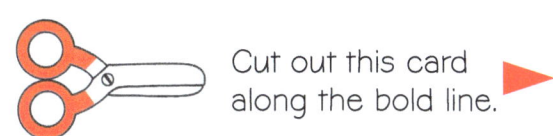

Cut out this card along the bold line. ▶

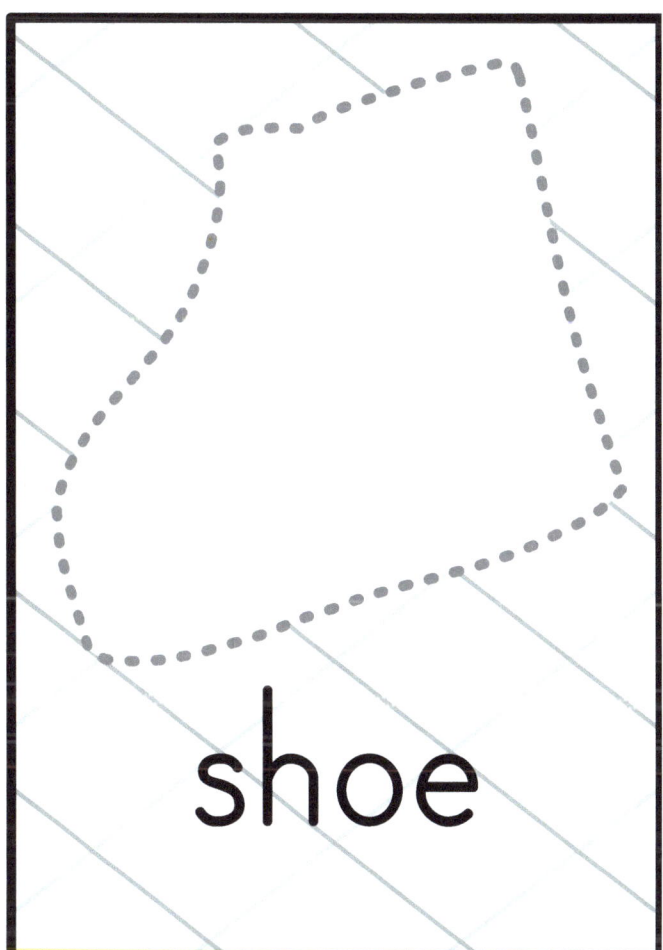

Cut out this pattern along the bold line. ▼

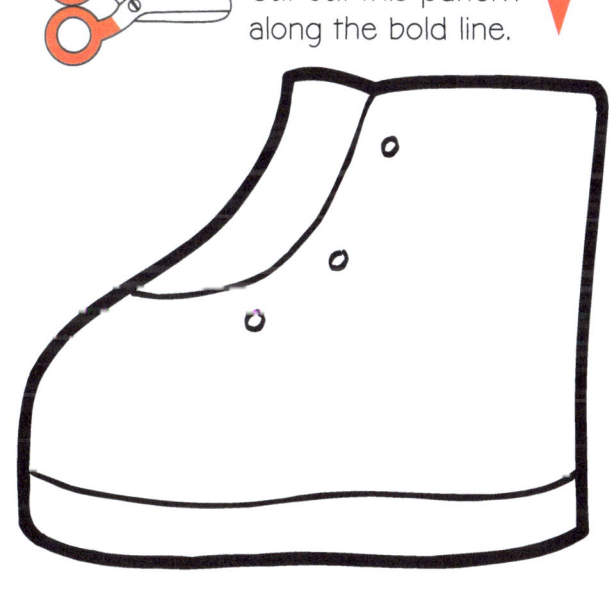

What You Will Need:

crayons   scissors
glue   yarn
buttons

What to Do:

1. Trace the dotted line.
2. Color and cut out the card.
3. Color and cut out the shoe pattern.
4. Glue the shoe cutout on the card.
5. Cut and glue yarn laces on the shoe.
6. Glue buttons on the shoe.

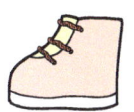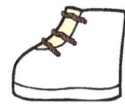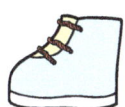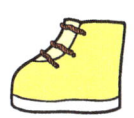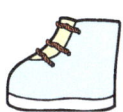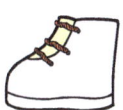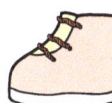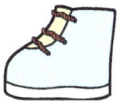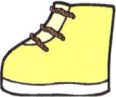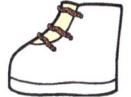

A Little Basket Project

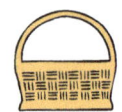 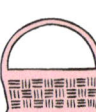 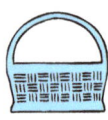 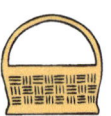 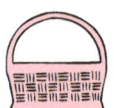

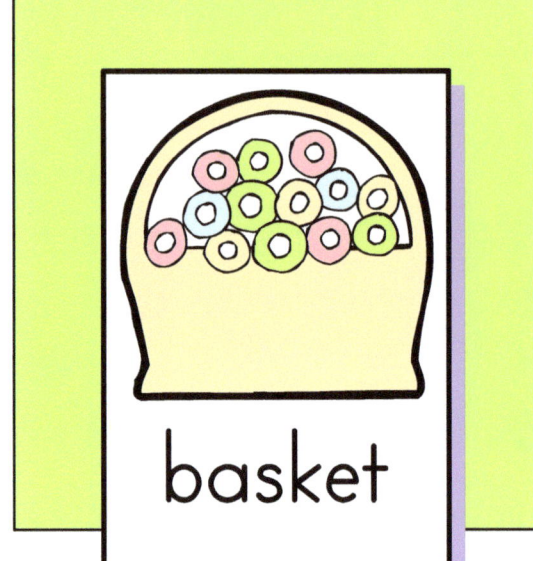

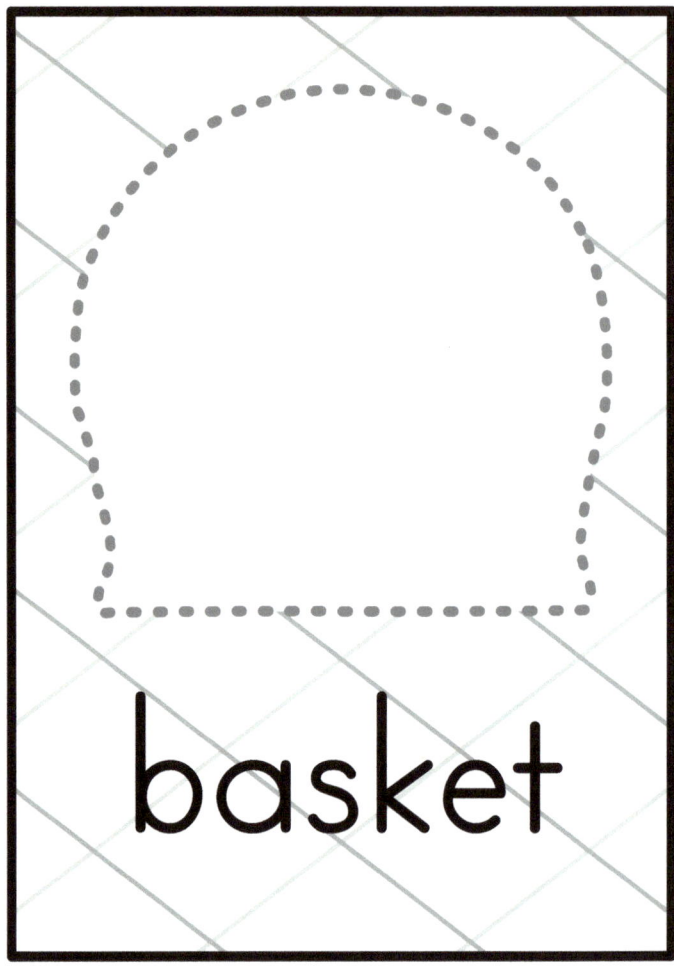

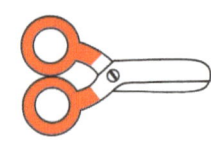 Cut out this card along the bold line. ▶

Cut out this pattern along the bold line. ▼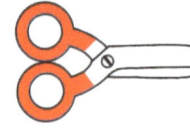

What You Will Need:

crayons   scissors
glue   cereal Os

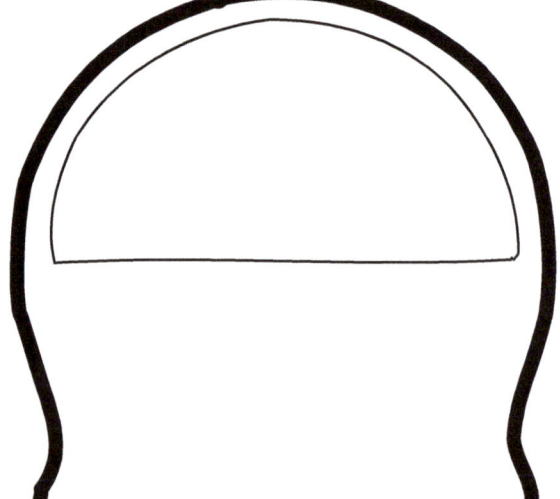

What to Do:

1. Trace the dotted line.
2. Color and cut out the card.
3. Color and cut out the basket pattern.
4. Glue the basket cutout on the card.
5. Glue cereal Os on the basket.

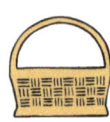 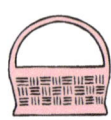 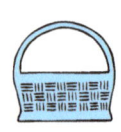 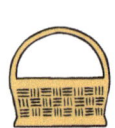 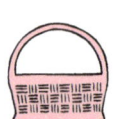 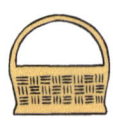

A Little Hat Project

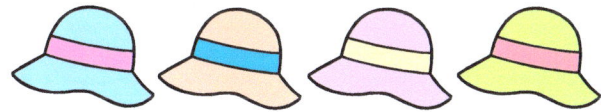

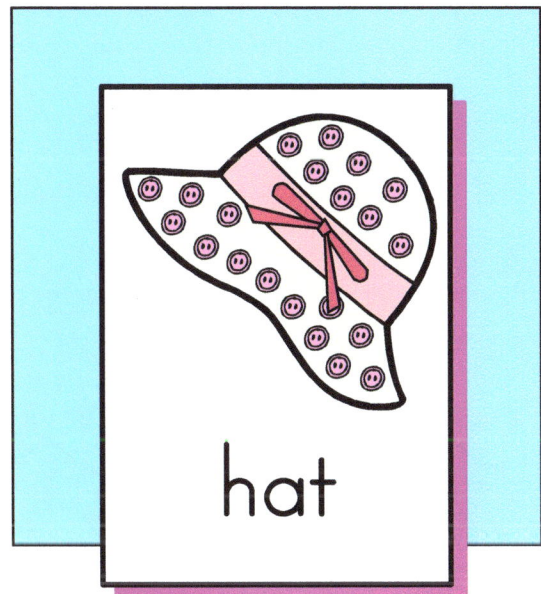

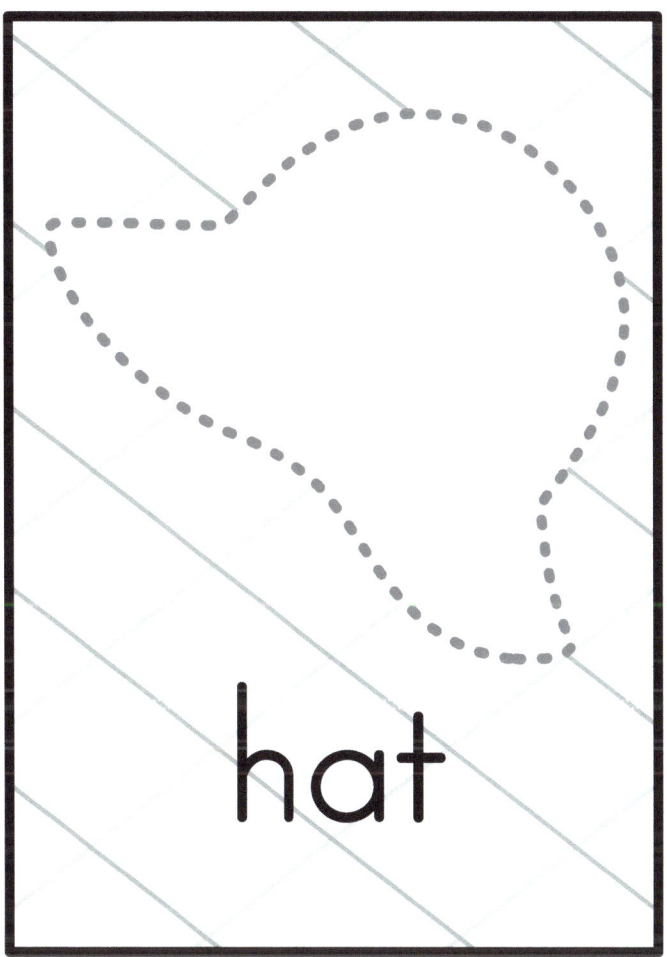

hat

Cut out this card along the bold line. ▶

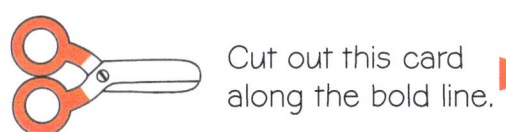

Cut out this pattern along the bold line. ▼

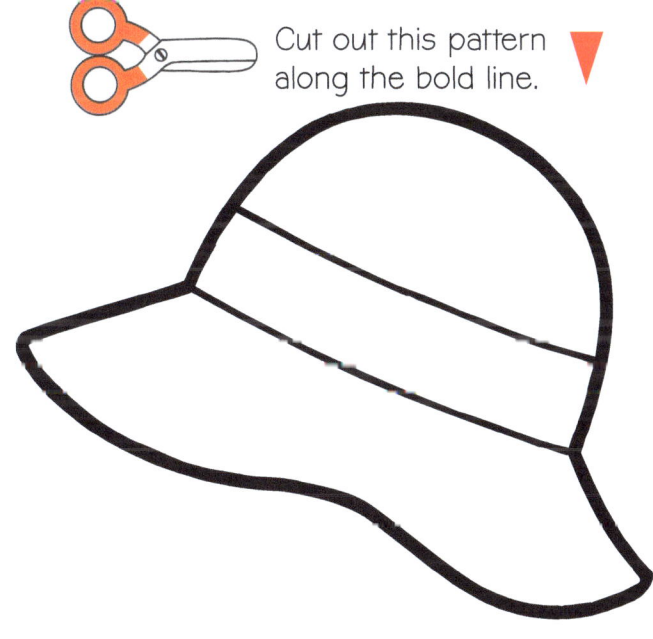

What You Will Need:

crayons   scissors

glue   small buttons

yarn or ribbon

What to Do:

1. Trace the dotted line.
2. Color and cut out the card.
3. Color and cut out the hat pattern.
4. Glue the hat cutout on the card.
5. Glue buttons on the hat.
6. Cut, tie, and glue a yarn or ribbon bow on the hat.

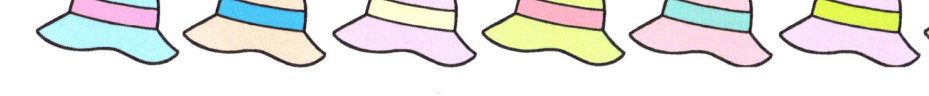

A Little Fish Project

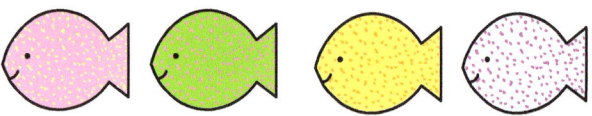

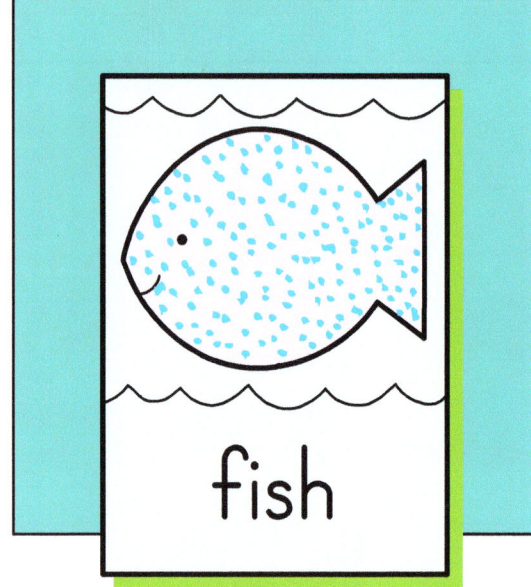

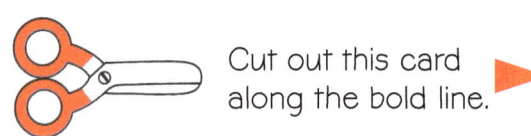

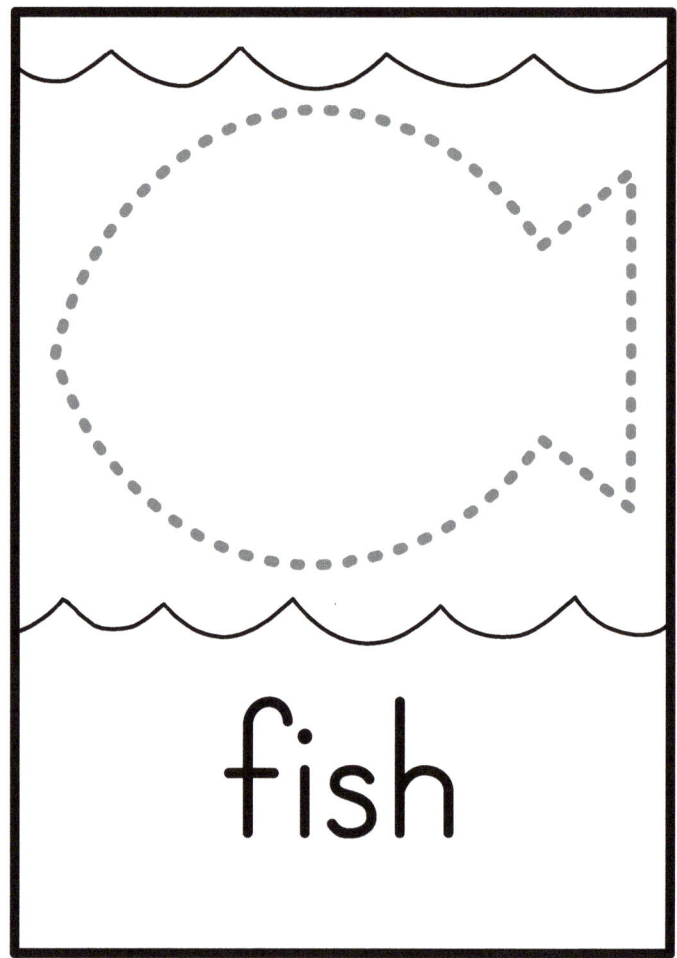

Cut out this card along the bold line. ▶

What You Will Need:

crayons   scissors
paint brush   glue
glitter

Cut out this pattern along the bold line. ▼

What to Do:

1. Trace the dotted line.
2. Color and cut out the card.
3. Color and cut out the fish pattern.
4. Glue the fish cutout on the card.
5. Apply glue with a paint brush, then sprinkle glitter on the fish.

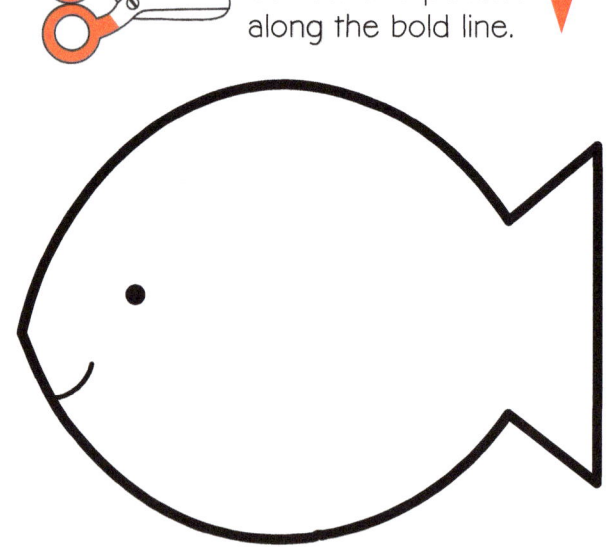

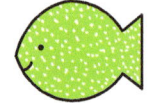 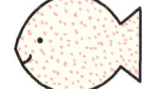 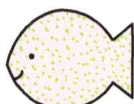 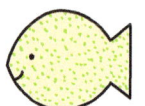 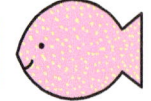 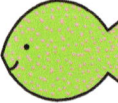 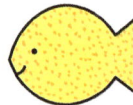 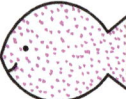 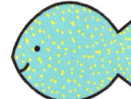

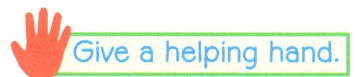 **Give a helping hand.**

A Little Shell Project

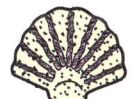 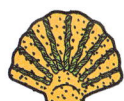 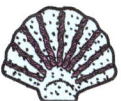 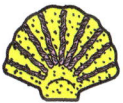 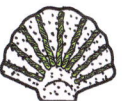

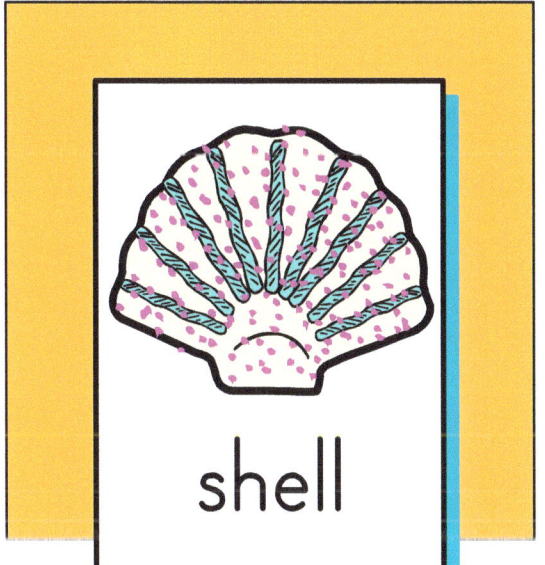

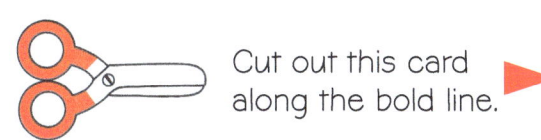
shell

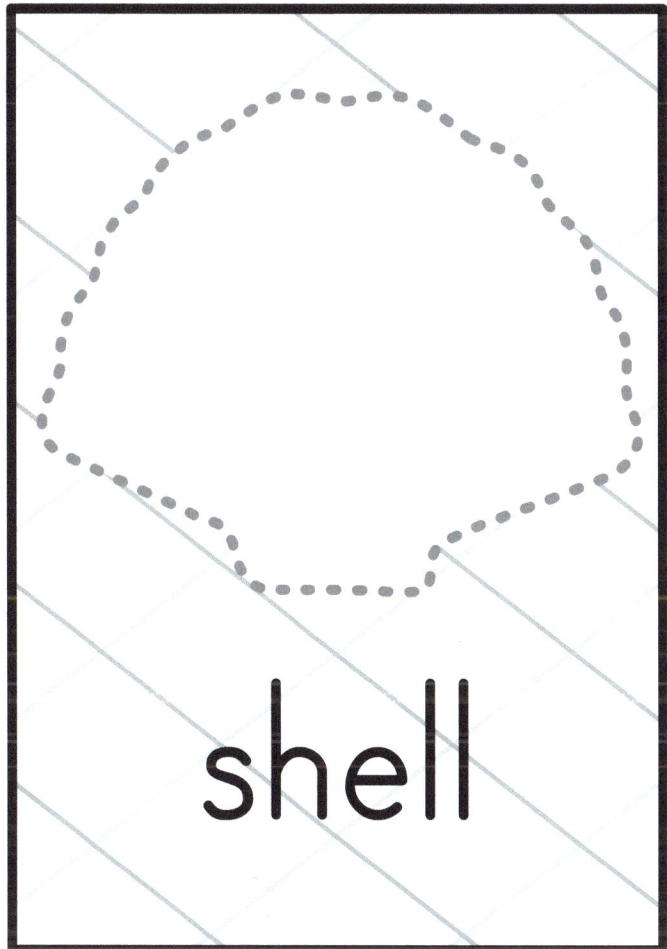
shell

Cut out this card along the bold line. ▶

Cut out this pattern along the bold line. ▼

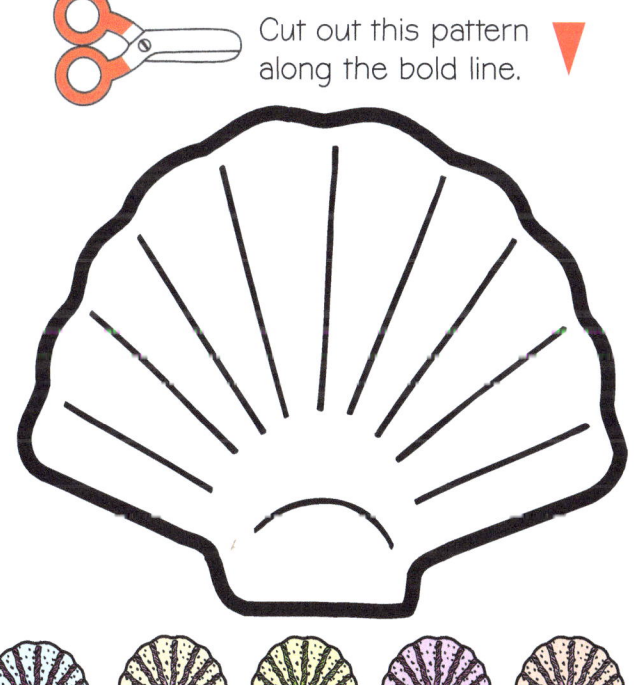

What You Will Need:

crayons   scissors
glue   pipe cleaners

What to Do:

1. Trace the dotted line.
2. Color and cut out the card.
3. Color and cut out the shell pattern.
4. Glue the shell cutout on the card.
5. Cut and glue pipe cleaners on the shell.

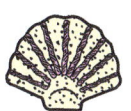 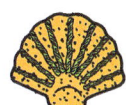 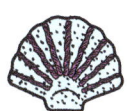 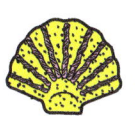 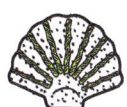 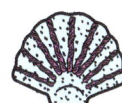 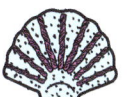 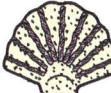 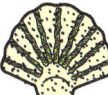 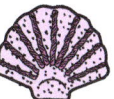 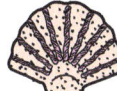

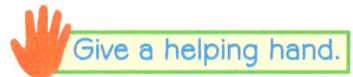 **Give a helping hand.**

A Little Mitten Project

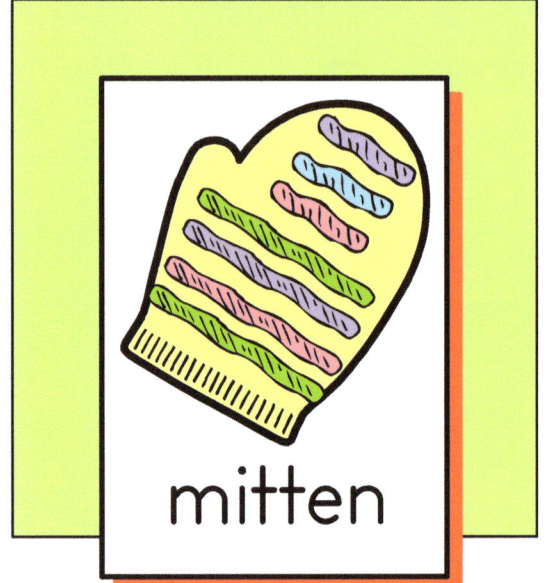

mitten

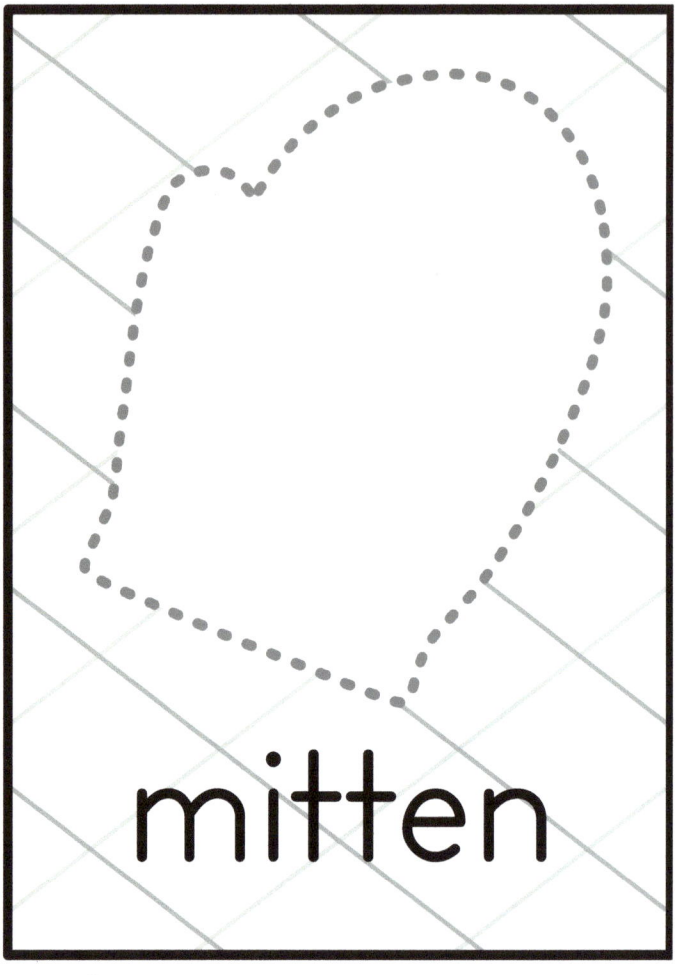

mitten

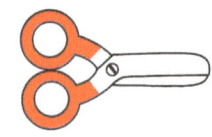 Cut out this card along the bold line. ▶

Cut out this pattern along the bold line. ▼

What You Will Need:
crayons   scissors
glue   yarn

What to Do:
1. Trace the dotted line.
2. Color and cut out the card.
3. Color and cut out the mitten pattern.
4. Glue the mitten cutout on the card.
5. Cut and glue yarn on the mitten.

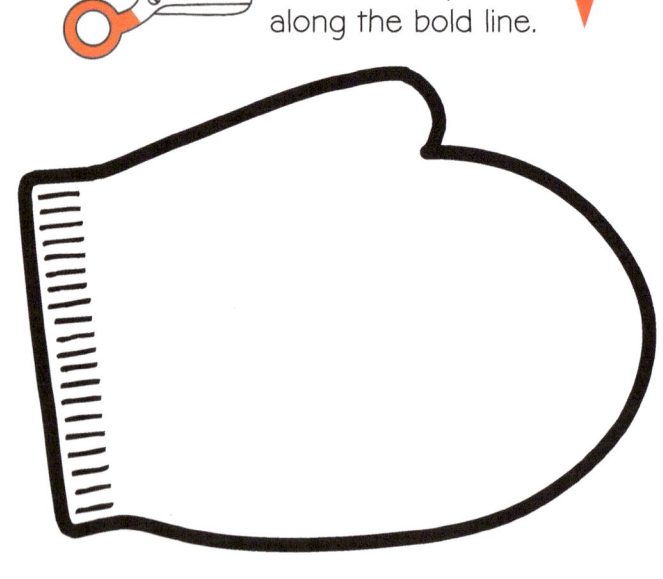

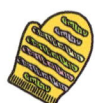 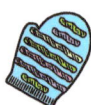 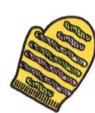 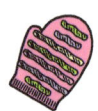 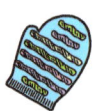 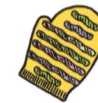

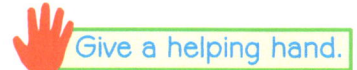
A Little Pumpkin Project

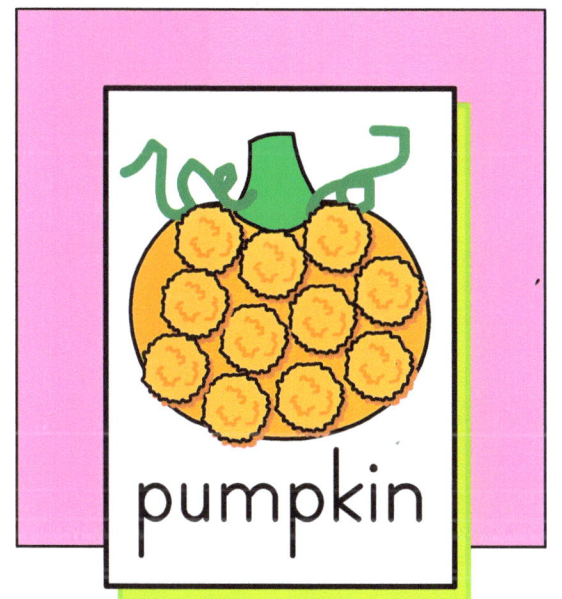

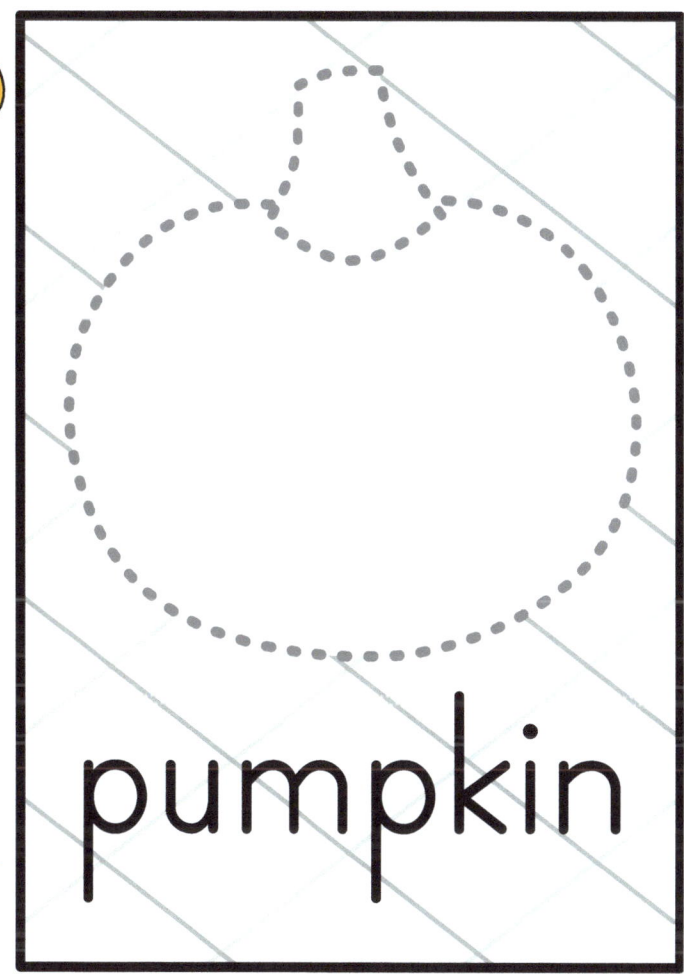

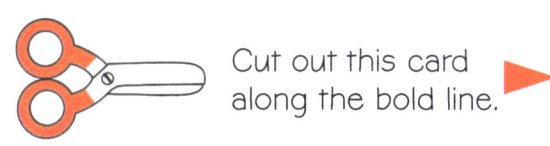 Cut out this card along the bold line. ▶

Cut out these patterns along the bold lines. ▼

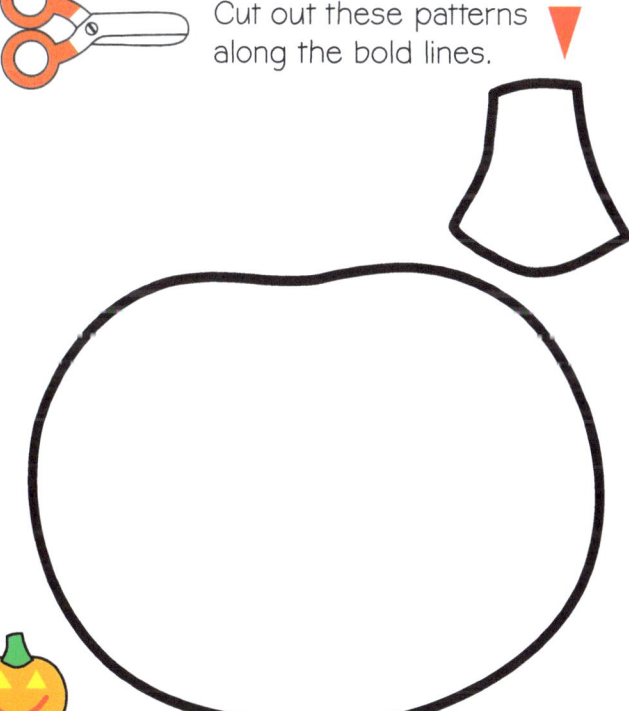

What You Will Need:

crayons   scissors
glue   orange pom poms
green yarn

What to Do:

1. Trace the dotted lines.
2. Color and cut out the card.
3. Color and cut out the pumpkin patterns.
4. Glue the pumpkin cutout then the stem on the card.
5. Glue pom poms on the pumpkin.
6. Cut and glue green yarn around the stem.

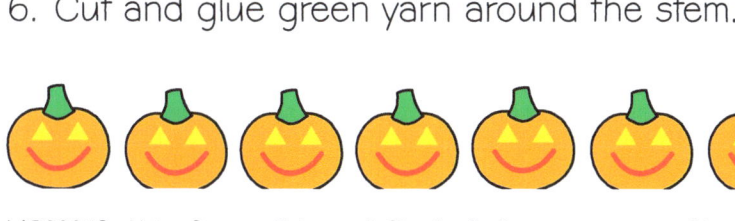

A Little Angel Project

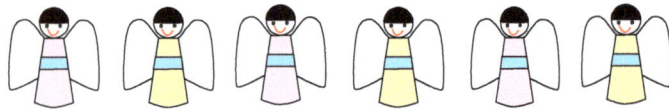

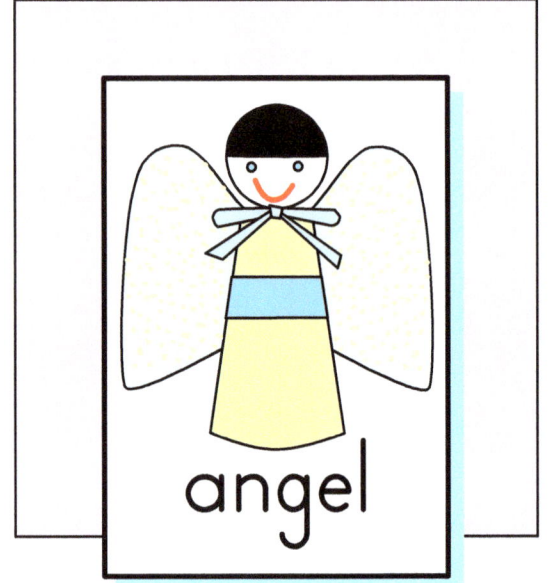

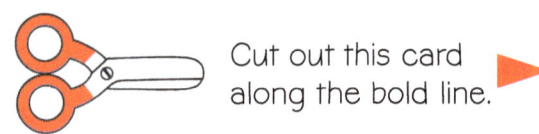

Cut out this card along the bold line. ▶

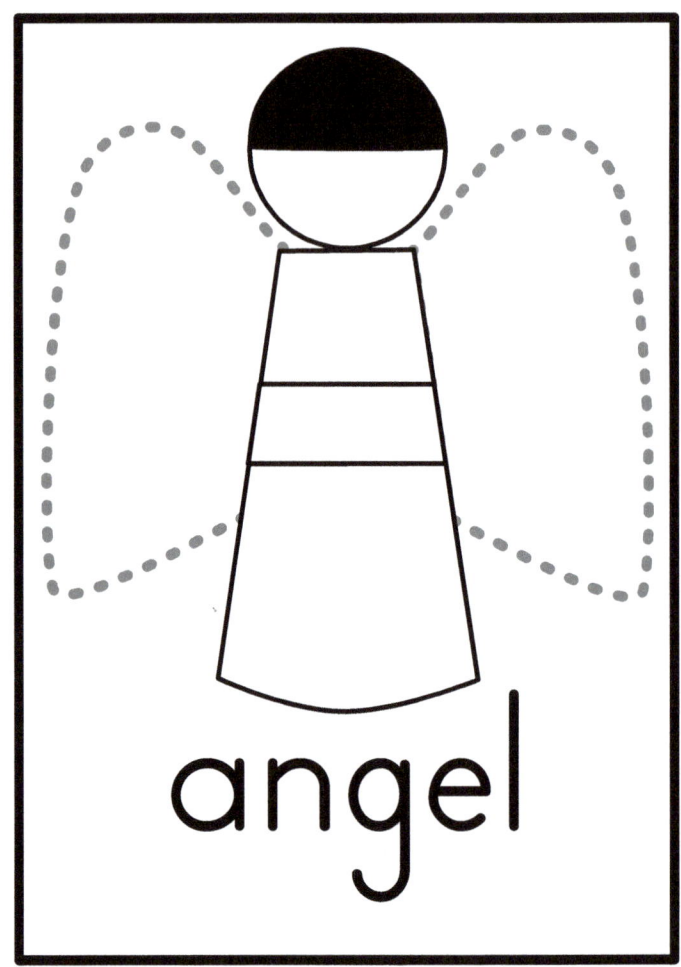

Cut out these patterns along the bold lines. ▼

What You Will Need:

crayons	scissors
glue	paint brush
glitter	ribbon

What to Do:

1. Trace the dotted lines.
2. Color and cut out the card.
3. Color and cut out the wings.
4. Glue the wings on the angel.
5. Apply glue with a paint brush, then sprinkle glitter on the wings.
6. Cut, tie, and glue a bow on the angel.

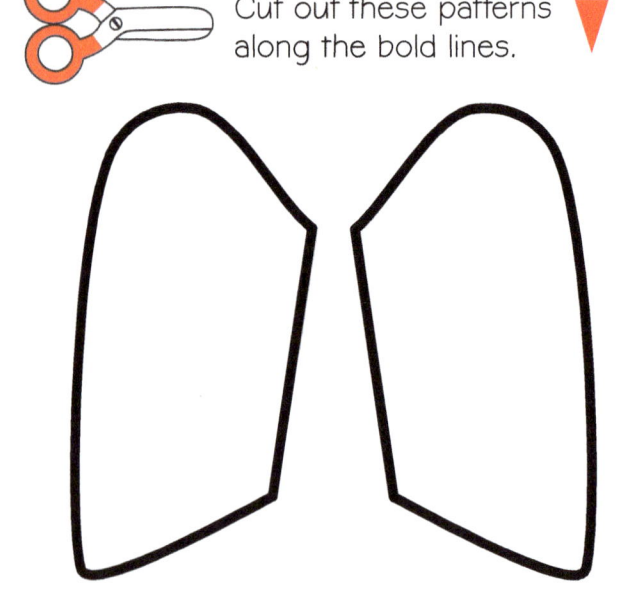

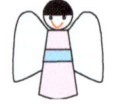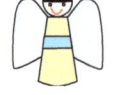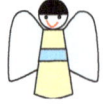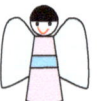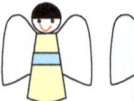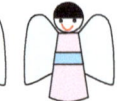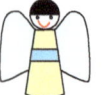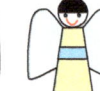

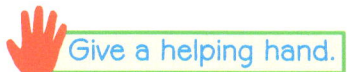 **Give a helping hand.**

A Little Flower Project

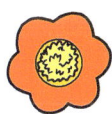 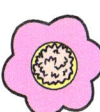   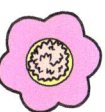

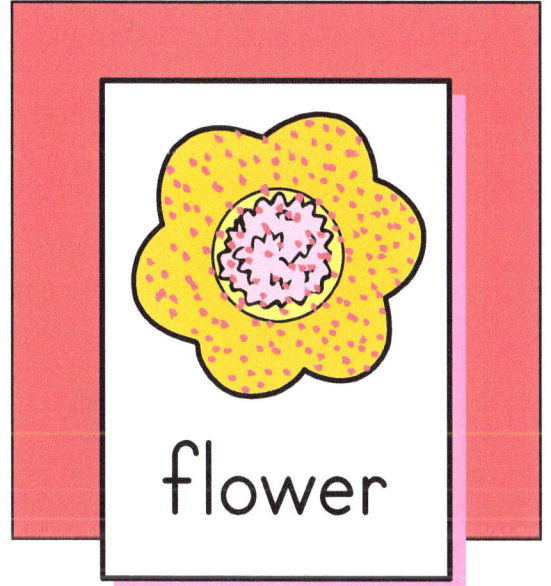

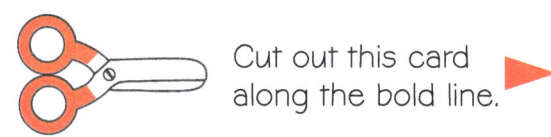

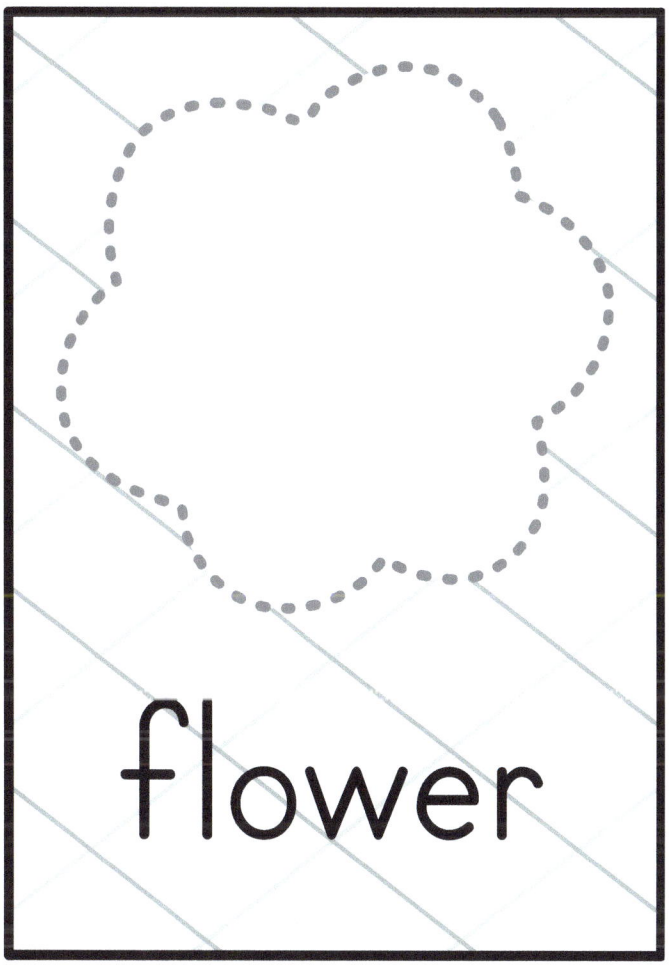

Cut out this card along the bold line. ▶

Cut out these patterns along the bold lines. ▼

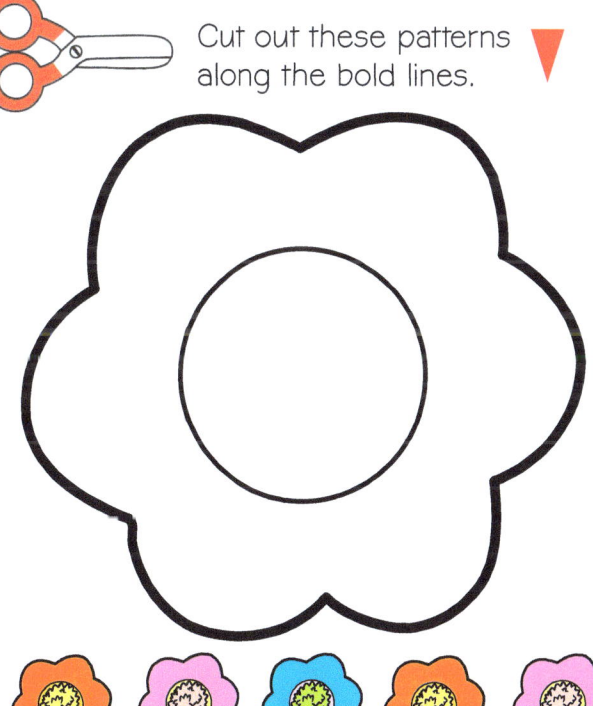

What You Will Need:

crayons   scissors
glue   pom pom

What to Do:

1. Trace the dotted line.
2. Color and cut out the card.
3. Color and cut out the flower pattern.
4. Glue the flower cutout on the card.
5. Glue a pom pom in the center of the flower.

 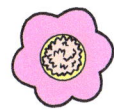 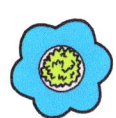  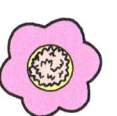 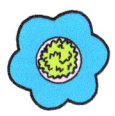  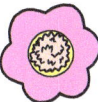 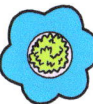  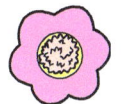

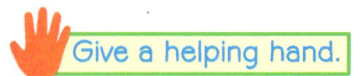 **Give a helping hand.**

A Little Sun Project

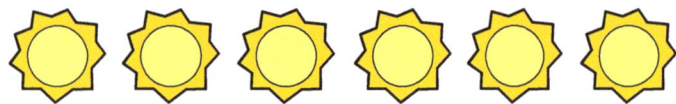

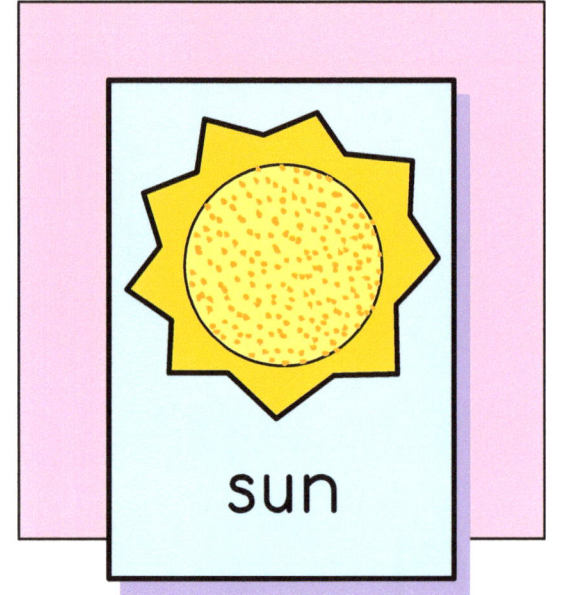

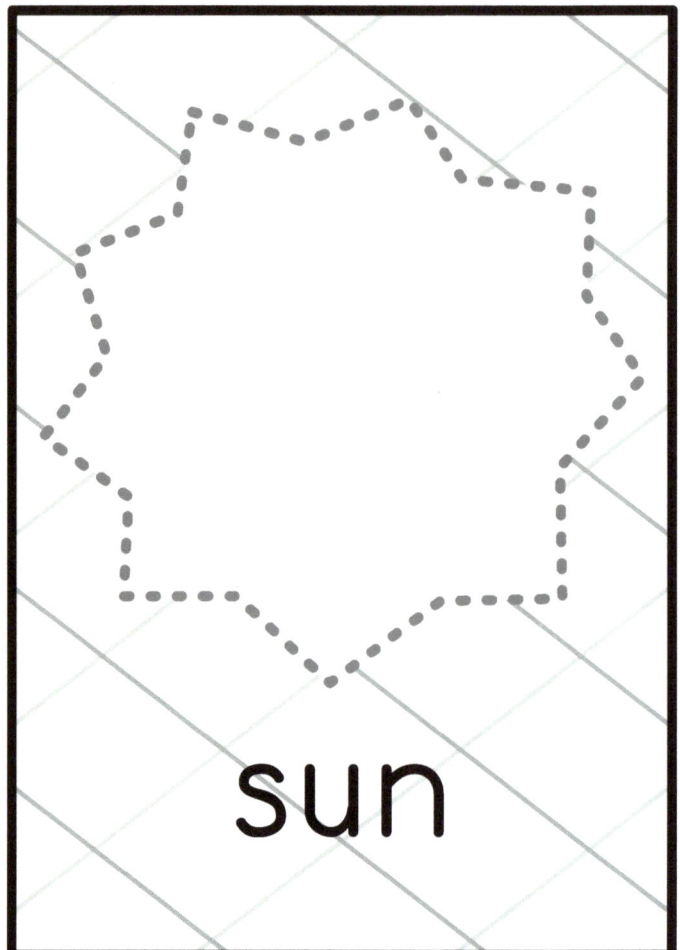

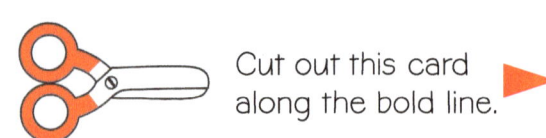 Cut out this card along the bold line.

Cut out this pattern along the bold line.

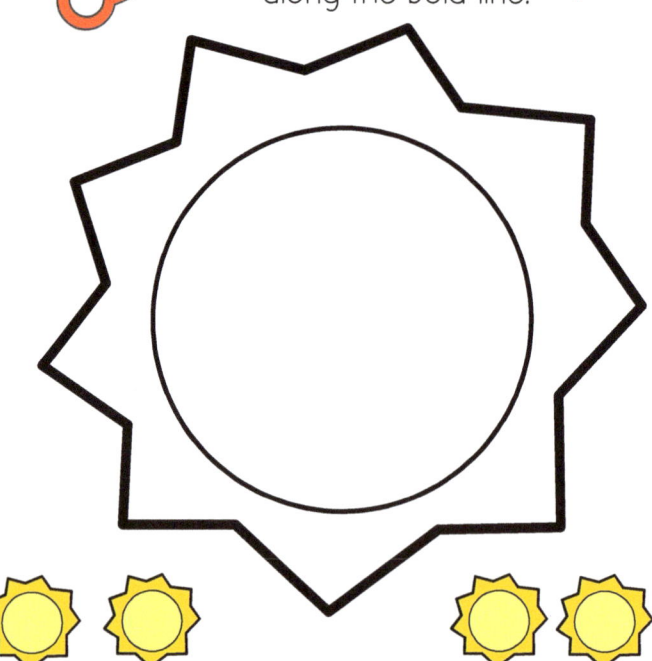

What You Will Need:

crayons   scissors
paint brush   glue
glitter

What to Do:

1. Trace the dotted line.
2. Color and cut out the card.
3. Color and cut out the sun pattern.
4. Glue the sun cutout on the card.
5. Apply glue with a paint brush, then sprinkle glitter on the sun.

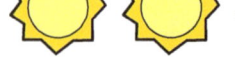

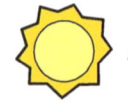      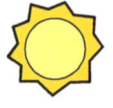 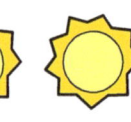

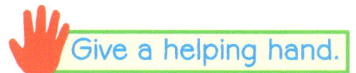
Give a helping hand.

A Little Whale Project

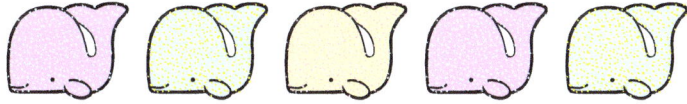

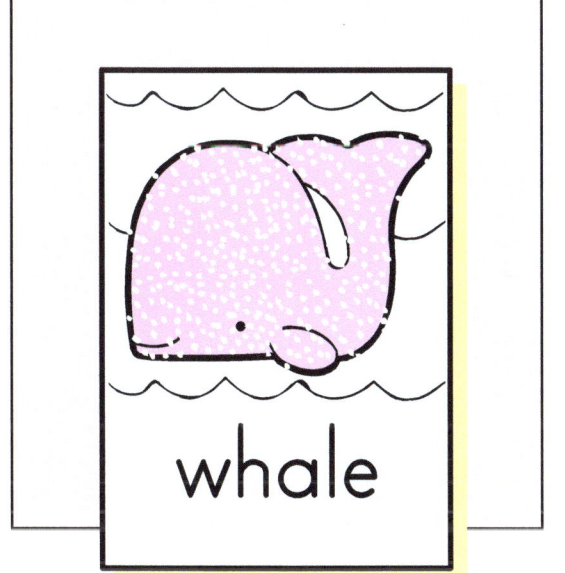

whale

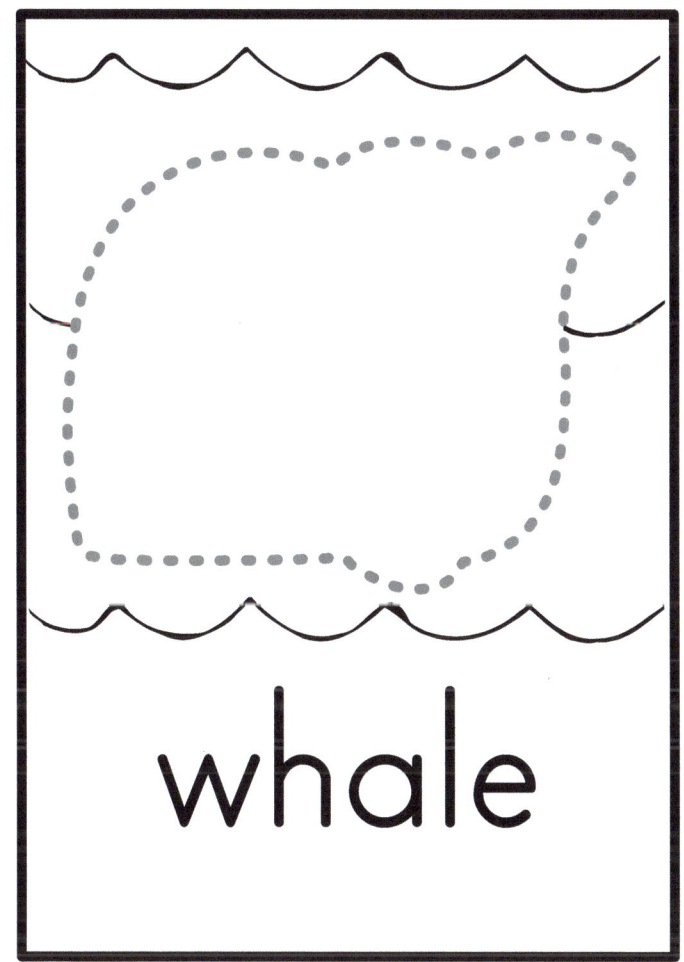

whale

Cut out this card along the bold line. ▶

Cut out this pattern along the bold line. ▼

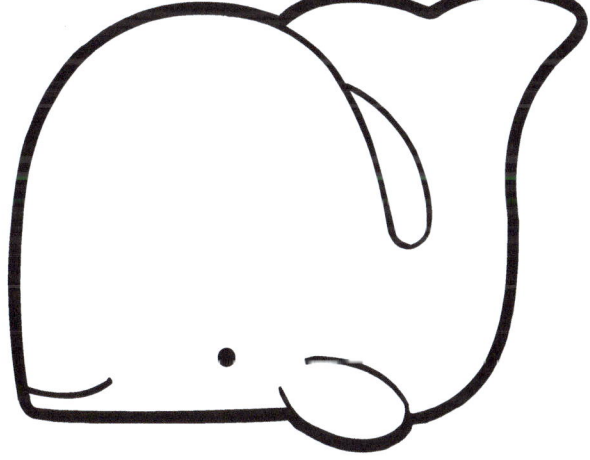

What You Will Need:

crayons   scissors
glue   glitter

What to Do:

1. Trace the dotted line.
2. Color and cut out the card.
3. Color and cut out the whale pattern.
4. Glue the whale cutout on the card.
5. Apply glue with a paint brush, then sprinkle glitter on the whale.

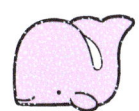 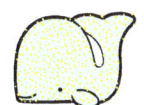 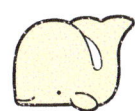 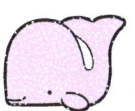 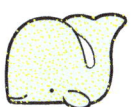 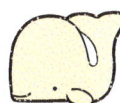 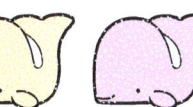 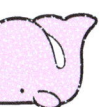 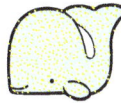 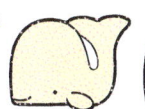 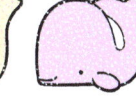

A Little Frog Project

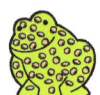   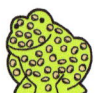

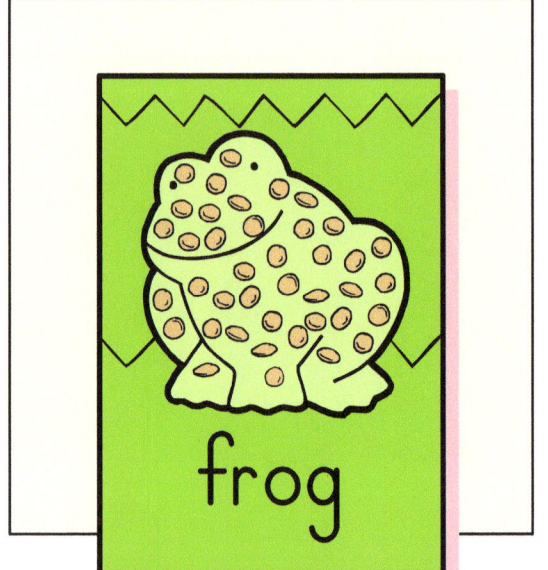

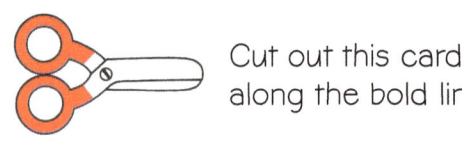

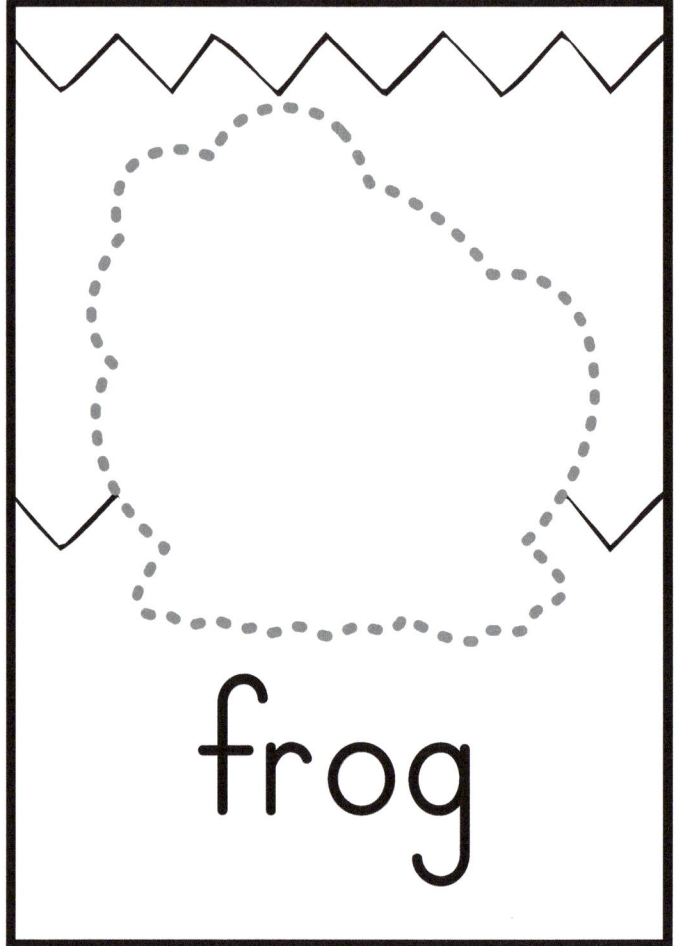

frog

Cut out this card along the bold line. ▶

Cut out this pattern along the bold line. ▼

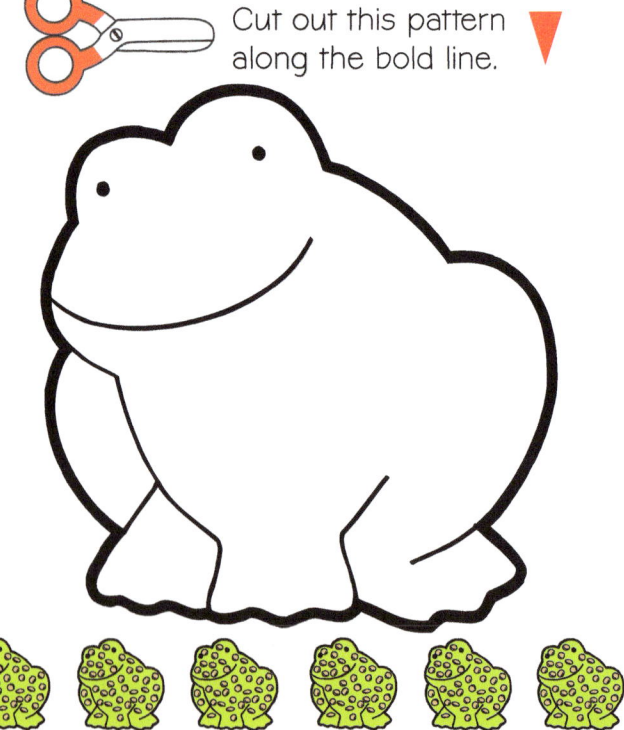

What You Will Need:

crayons   scissors
glue   dry beans

What to Do:

1. Trace the dotted line.
2. Color and cut out the card.
3. Color and cut out the frog pattern.
4. Glue the frog cutout on the card.
5. Glue dry beans on the frog.

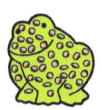 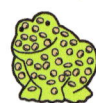 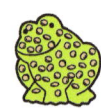 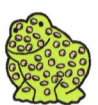 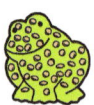 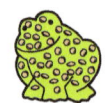 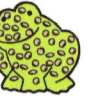 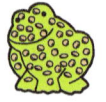 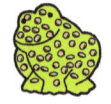 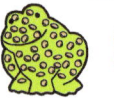 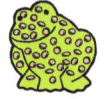

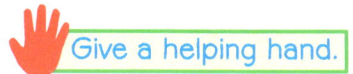

A Little Rabbit Project

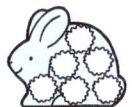 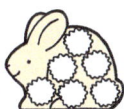 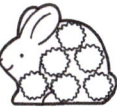 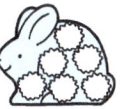 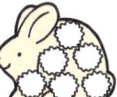

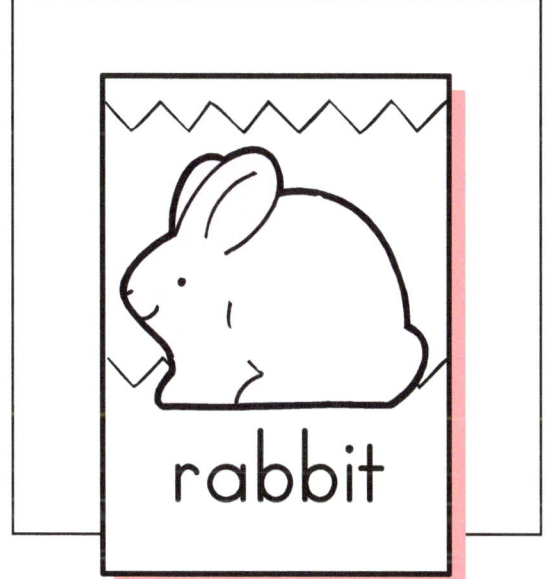

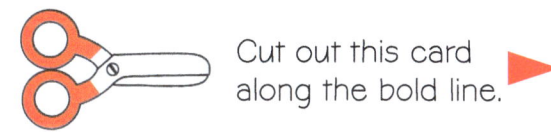

rabbit

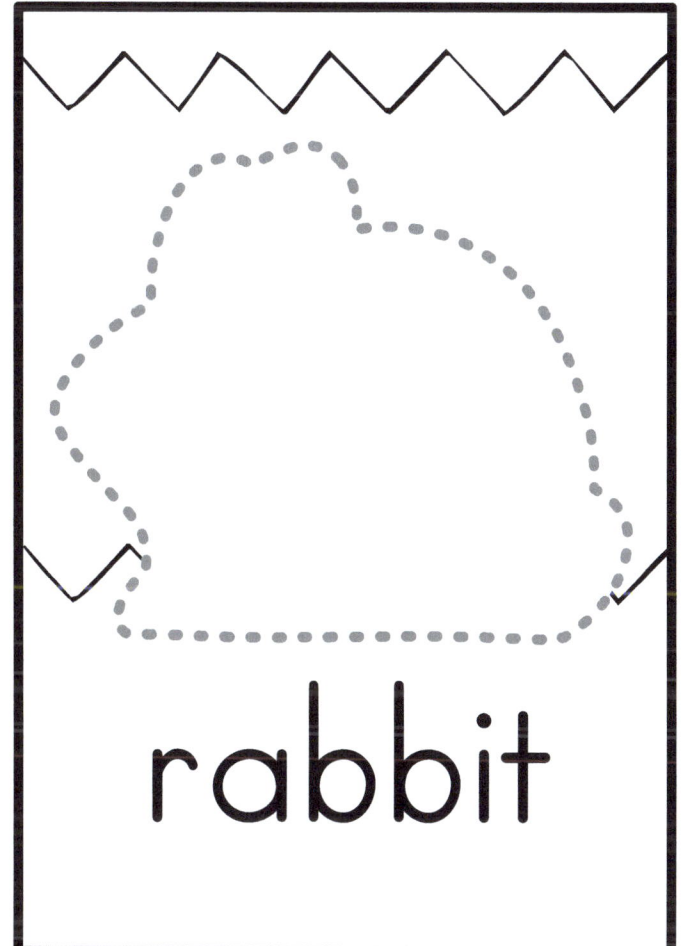

rabbit

Cut out this card
along the bold line. ▶

Cut out this pattern
along the bold line. ▼

What You Will Need:

crayons   scissors
glue   cotton balls

What to Do:

1. Trace the dotted line.
2. Color and cut out the card.
3. Color and cut out the rabbit pattern.
4. Glue the rabbit cutout on the card.
5. Glue cotton balls on the rabbit.

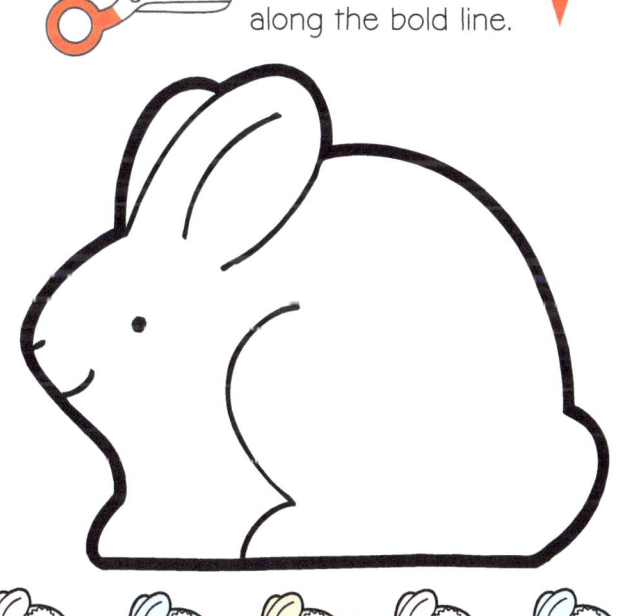

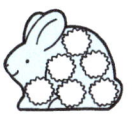 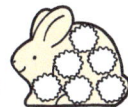 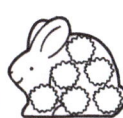 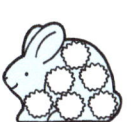 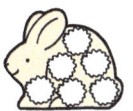 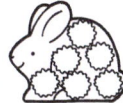 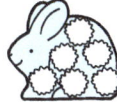 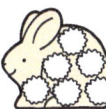 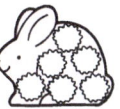 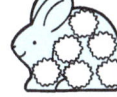

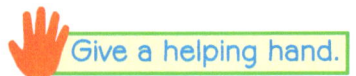 Give a helping hand.

A Little Buttefly Project

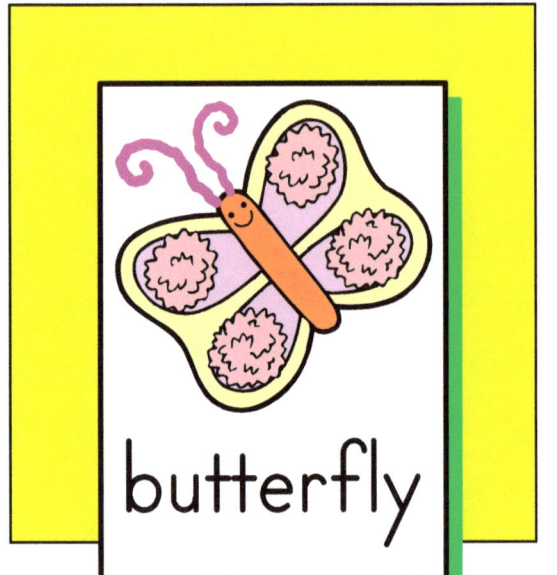

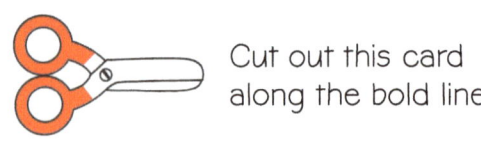 butterfly

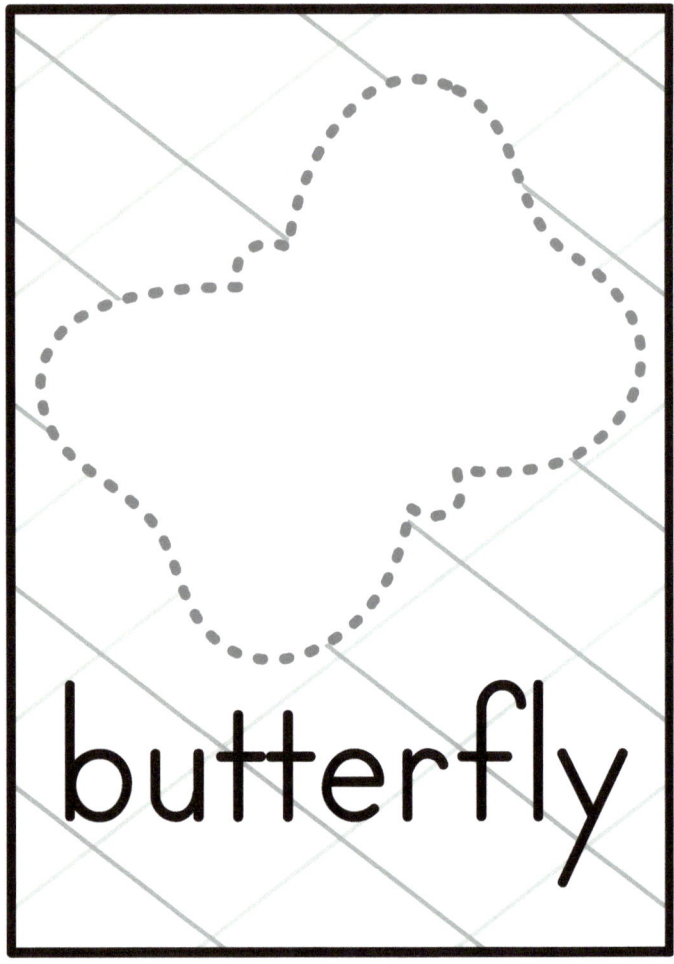
butterfly

Cut out this card along the bold line. ▶

Cut out this pattern along the bold line. ▼

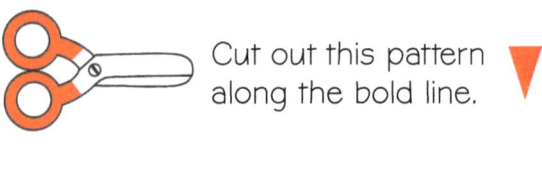

What You Will Need:

crayons	scissors
glue	4 pom poms
pipe cleaner	

What to Do:

1. Trace the dotted line.
2. Color and cut out the card.
3. Color and cut out the butterfly pattern.
4. Glue the butterfly cutout on the card.
5. Glue pom poms on the butterfly.
6. Cut and glue two pipe cleaner antennae on the butterfly.

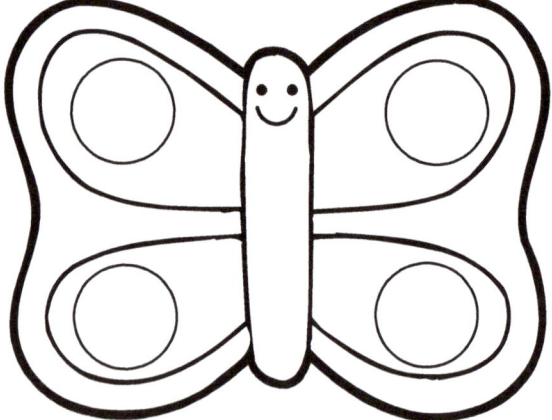

        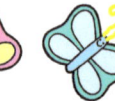   

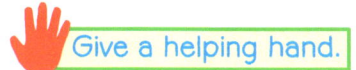
A Little Chick Project

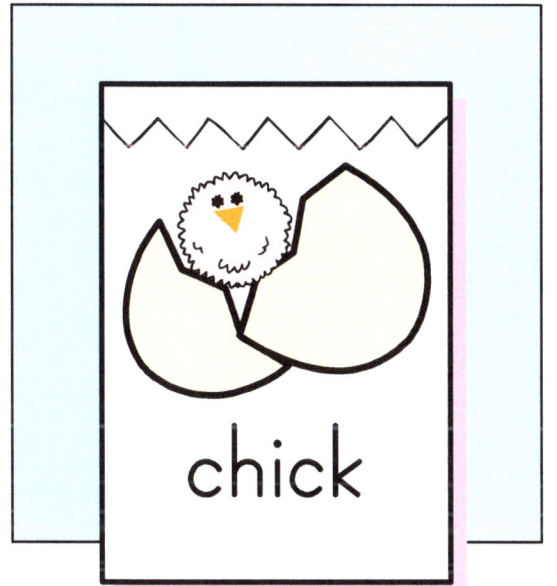

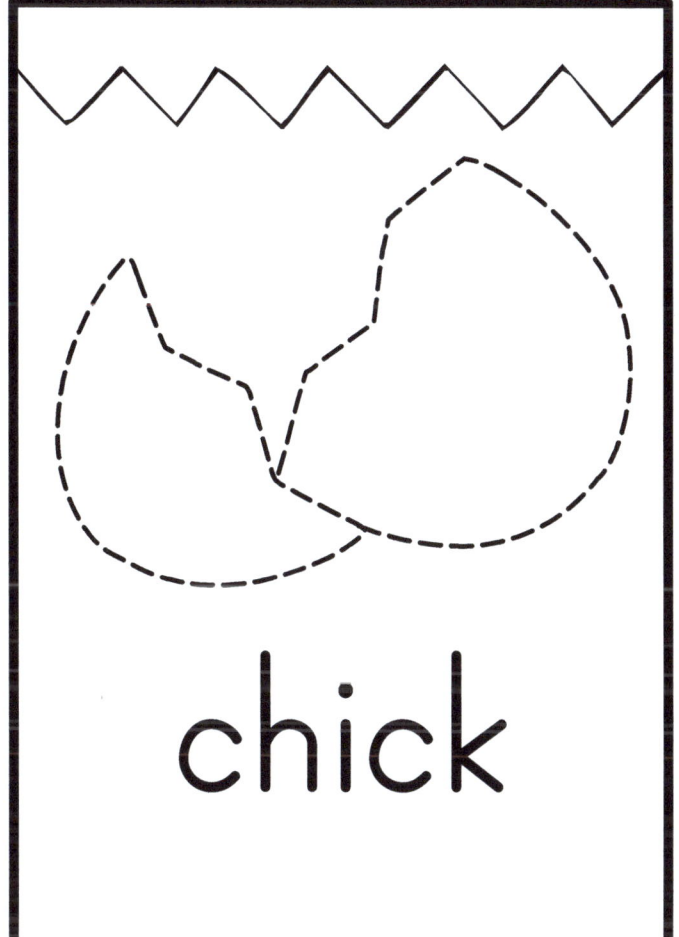

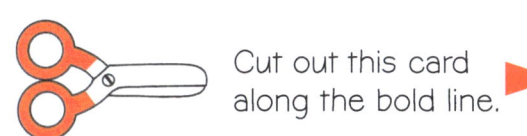 Cut out this card along the bold line.

Cut out these patterns along the bold lines.

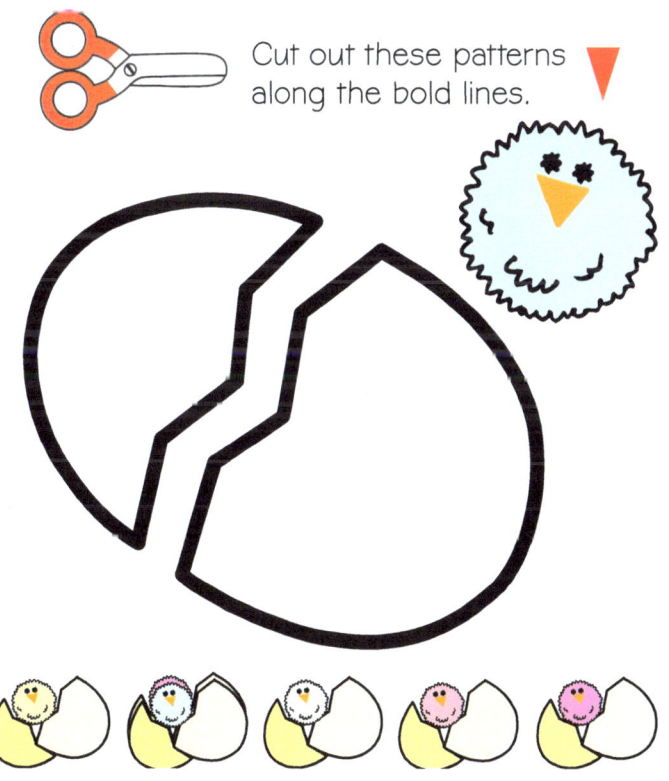

What You Will Need:

crayons   scissors   glue   pom pom
permanent marker
orange construction paper

What to Do:

1. Trace the dotted lines.
2. Color and cut out the card.
3. Color and cut out the egg patterns.
4. Glue the egg cutouts on the card.
5. Glue a pom pom chick on the card.
6. Use a permanent marker to draw two eyes on the pom pom.
7. Cut and glue an orange triangle beak on the pom pom as shown above.

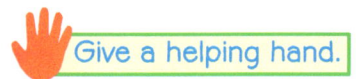 Give a helping hand.

A Little Pinwheel Project

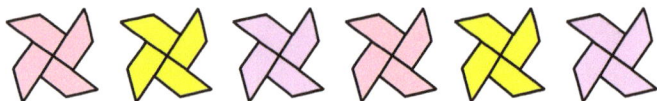

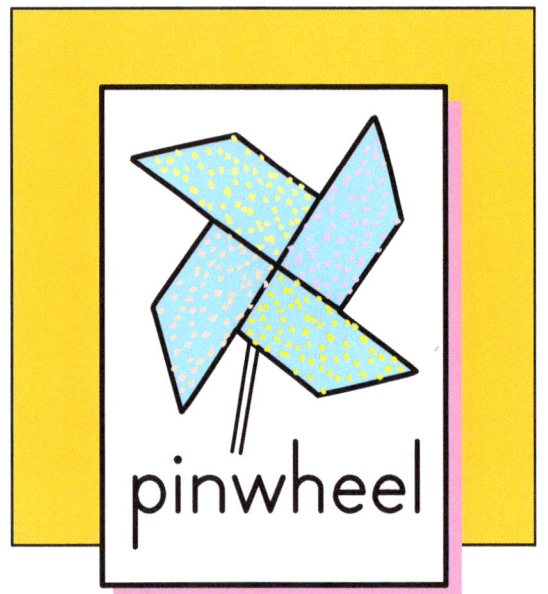

pinwheel

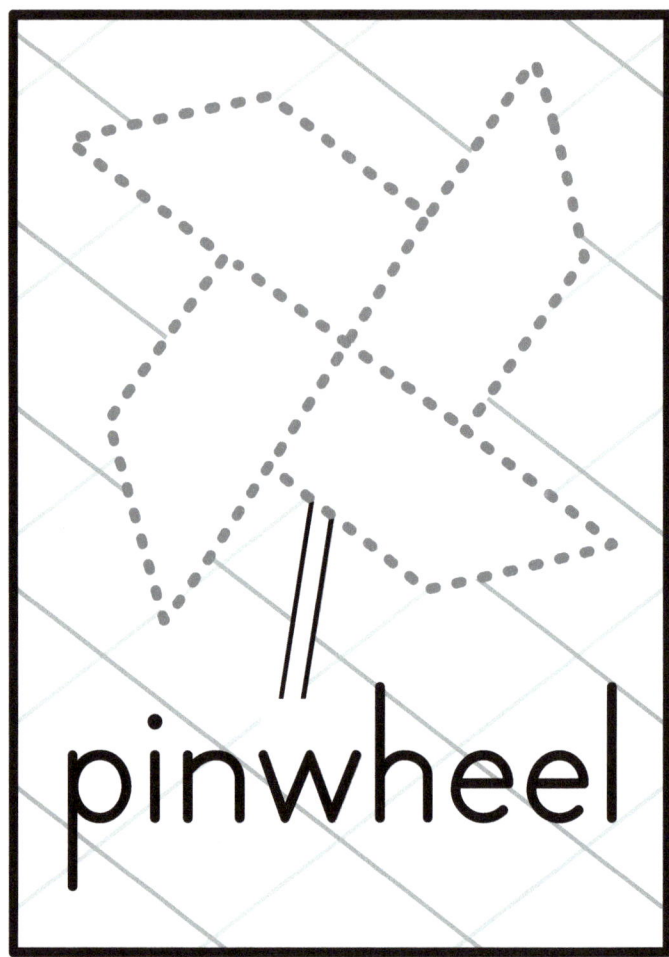

pinwheel

Cut out this card along the bold line. ▶

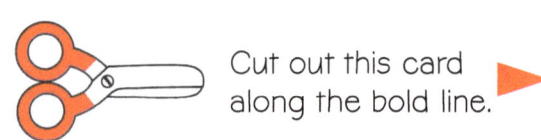

Cut out these patterns along the bold lines. ▼

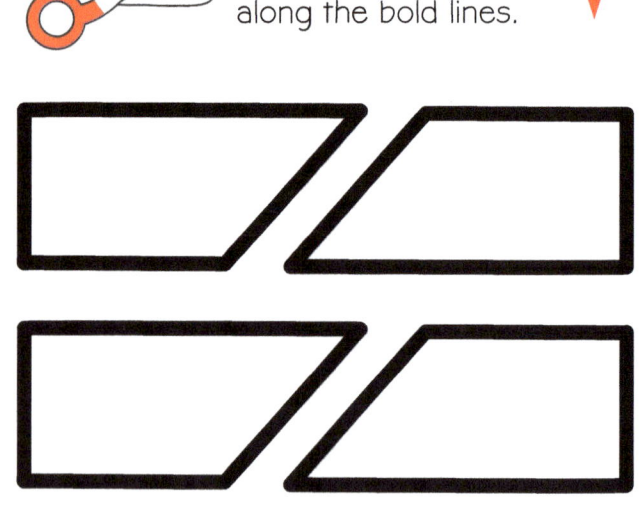

What You Will Need:

crayons	scissors
paint brush	glue
glitter	

What to Do:

1. Trace the dotted lines.
2. Color and cut out the card.
3. Color and cut out the pinwheel patterns.
4. Glue the pinwheel cutouts on the card.
5. Apply glue with a paint brush, then sprinkle glitter on the pinwheel.

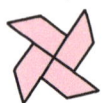  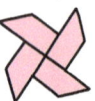  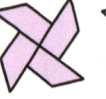 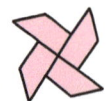

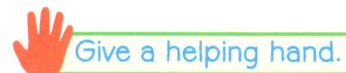 **Give a helping hand.**

A Little Gingerbread Man Project

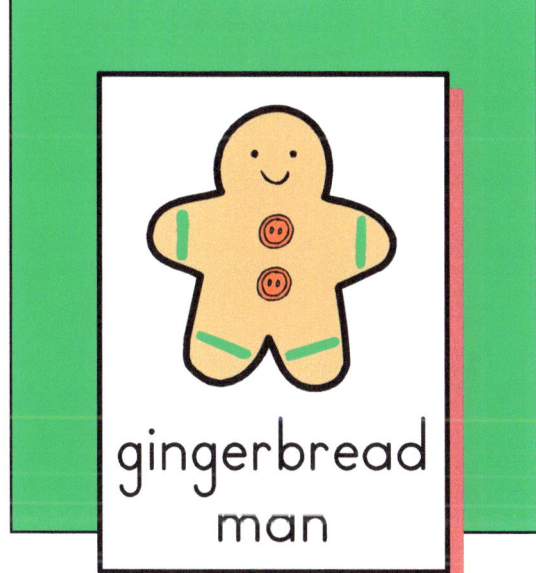

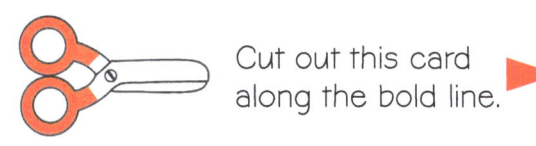
gingerbread man

Cut out this card along the bold line. ▶

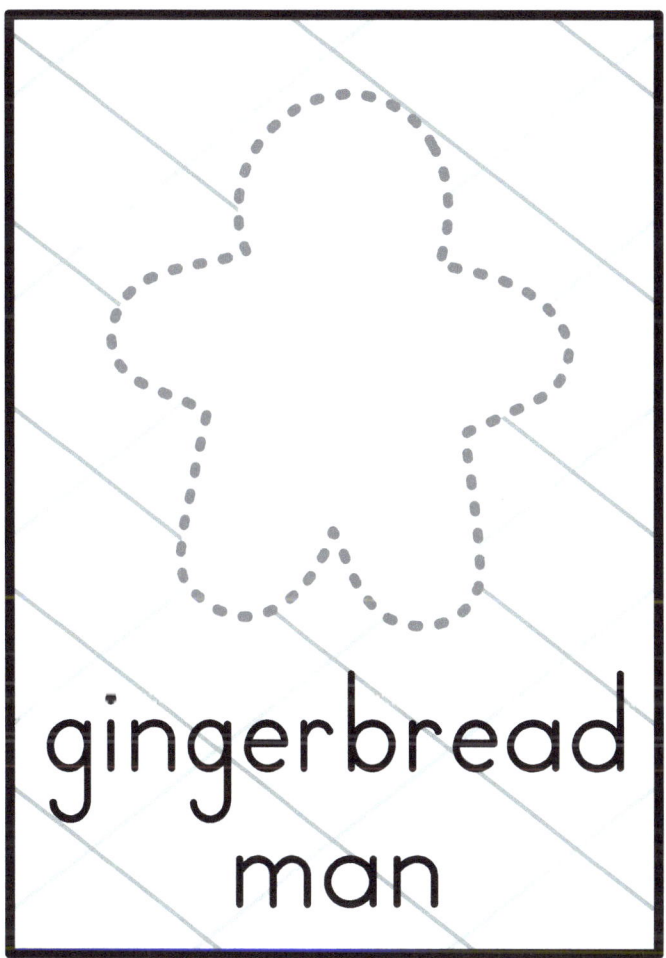
gingerbread man

Cut out this pattern along the bold line. ▼

What You Will Need:

crayons   scissors
glue   two pom poms
yarn

What to Do:

1. Trace the dotted line.
2. Color and cut out the card.
3. Color and cut out the gingerbread man pattern.
4. Glue the gingerbread man cutout on the card.
5. Glue pom pom buttons on the gingerbread man.
6. Cut and glue yarn cuffs on the gingerbread man.

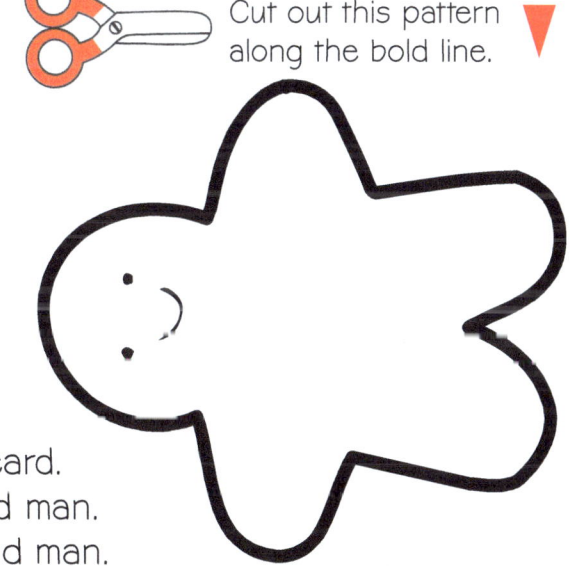

      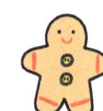 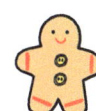 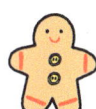  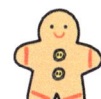

LAB20043 · Using Crayons, Scissors & Glue for Crafts   31   ©2010 Little Acorn Books

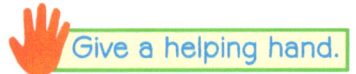

A Little Bird Project

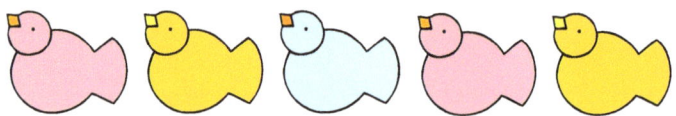

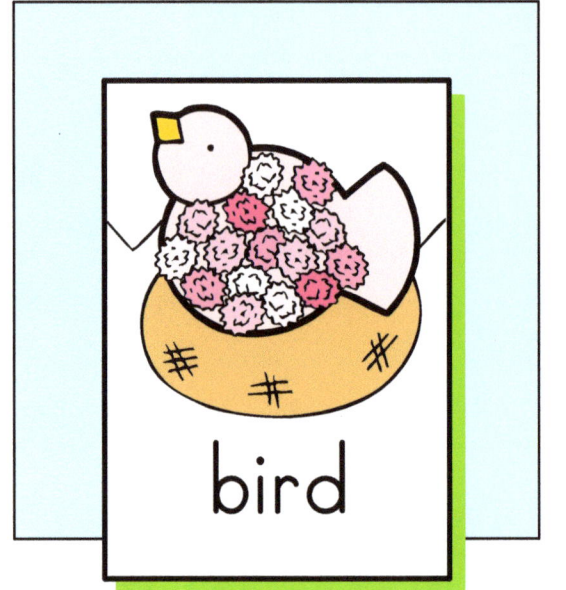

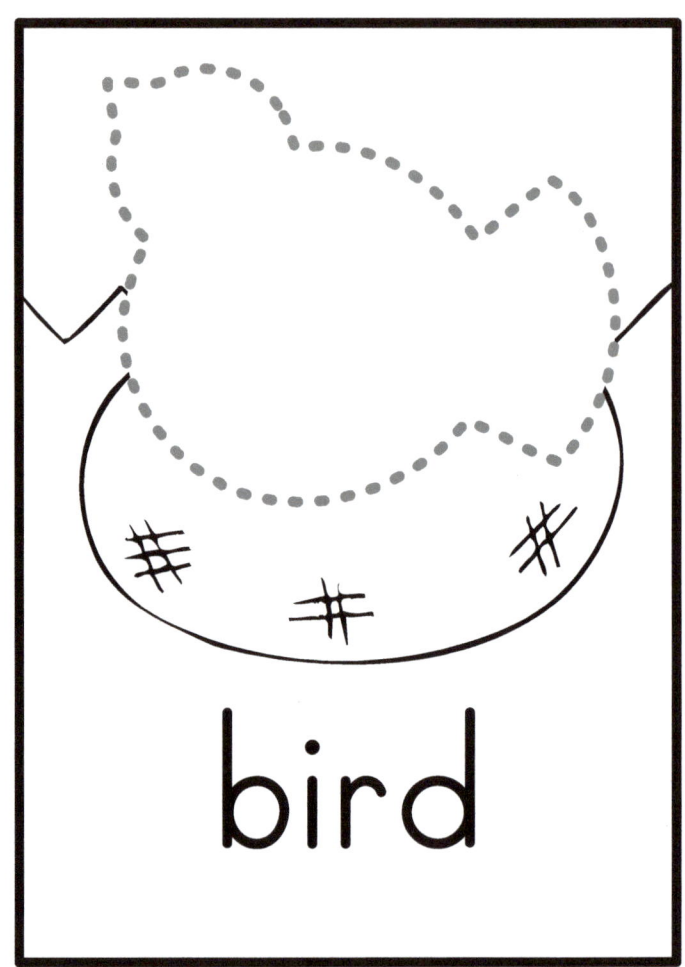

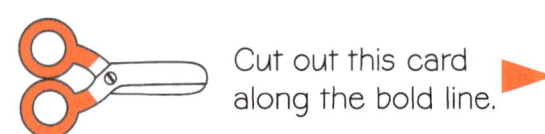 Cut out this card along the bold line. ▶

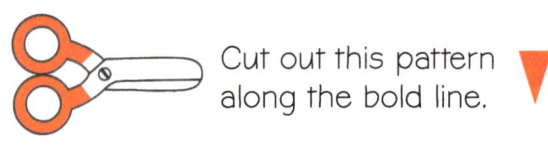 Cut out this pattern along the bold line. ▼

What You Will Need:

crayons   scissors
glue   small pom poms

What to Do:

1. Trace the dotted line.
2. Color and cut out the card.
3. Color and cut out the bird pattern.
4. Glue the bird cutout on the card.
5. Glue pom poms on the bird.

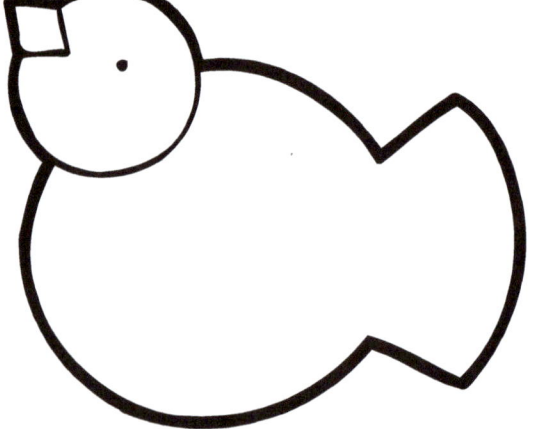

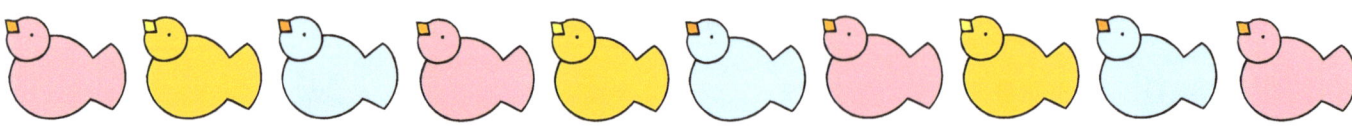

 Give a helping hand.

A Little Chameleon Project

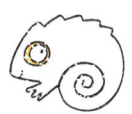 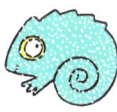 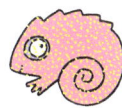 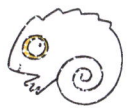 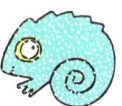

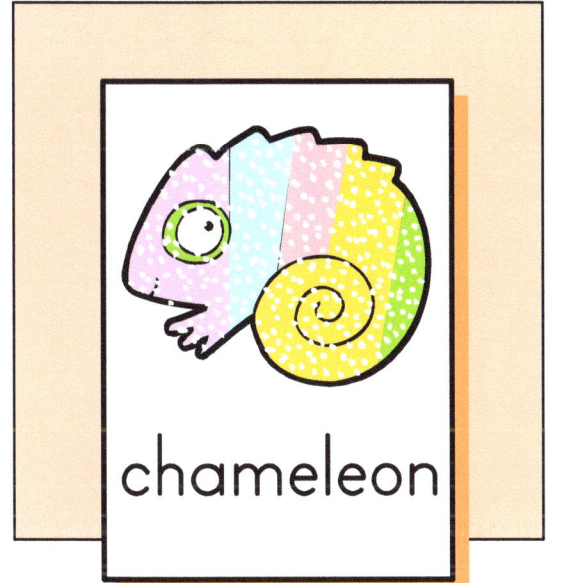

chameleon

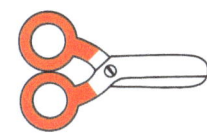 Cut out this card along the bold line. ▶

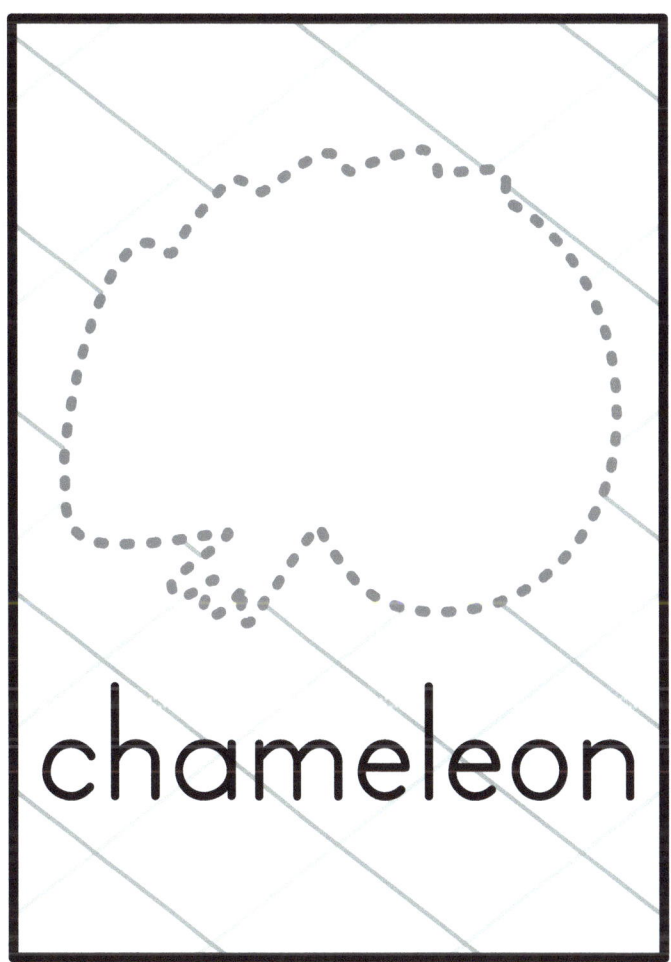

chameleon

Cut out this pattern along the bold line. ▼

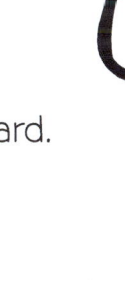

What You Will Need:

crayons   scissors
paint brush   glue
glitter

What to Do:

1. Trace the dotted line.
2. Color and cut out the card.
3. Color and cut out the chameleon pattern.
4. Glue the chameleon cutout on the card.
5. Apply glue with a paint brush, then sprinkle glitter on the chameleon.

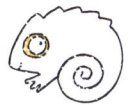 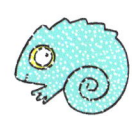 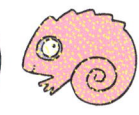 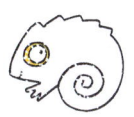 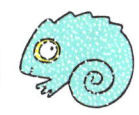 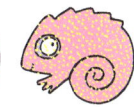 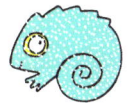 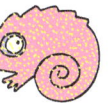 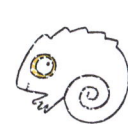 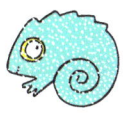 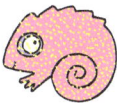 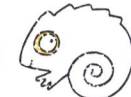

 **Give a helping hand.**

A Little Snowman Project

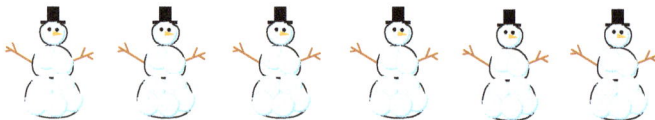

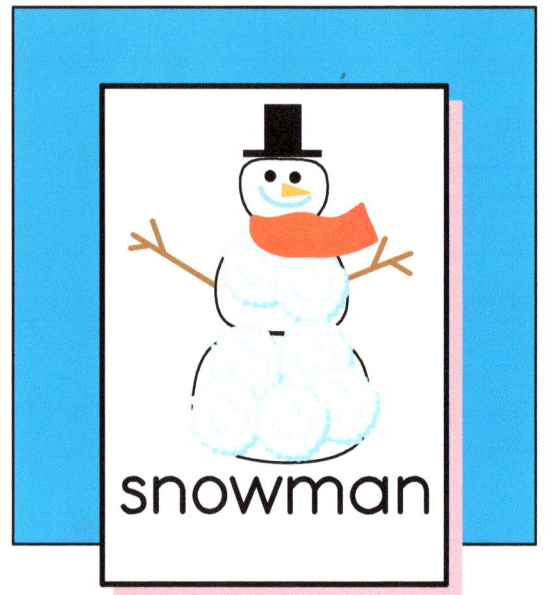

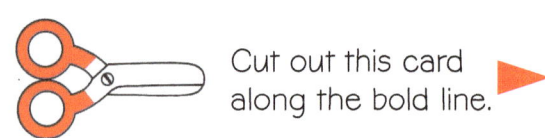 Cut out this card along the bold line. ▶

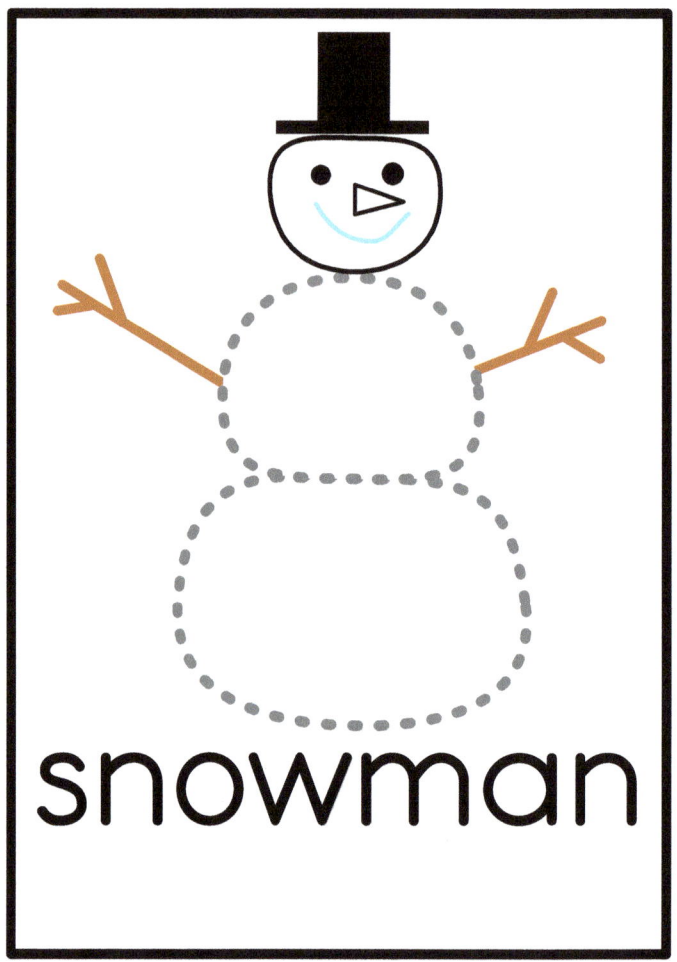

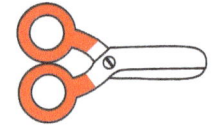 Cut out these patterns along the bold lines.

What You Will Need:

crayons and a black marker
scissors   glue
cotton balls   red construction paper

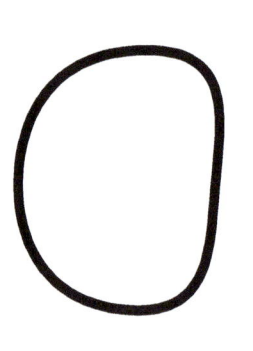 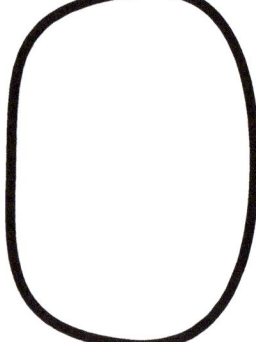

What to Do:

1. Trace the dotted lines.
2. Color and cut out the card.
3. Color and cut out the snowman patterns.
4. Glue the snowman cutouts on the card.
5. Glue cotton balls on the snowman.
6. Cut and glue a red scarf around the snowman's neck.

     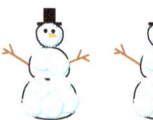 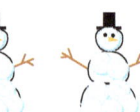     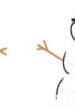

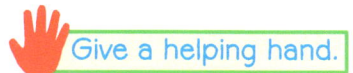

A Little Tulip Project

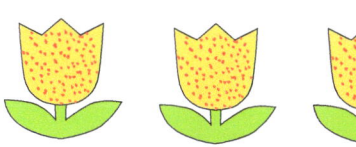

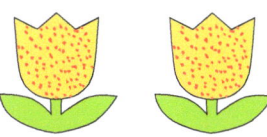

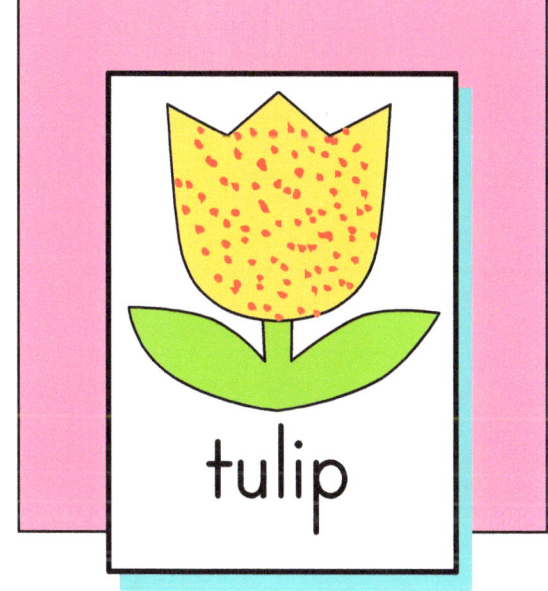

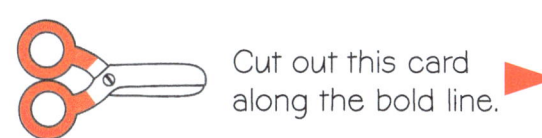

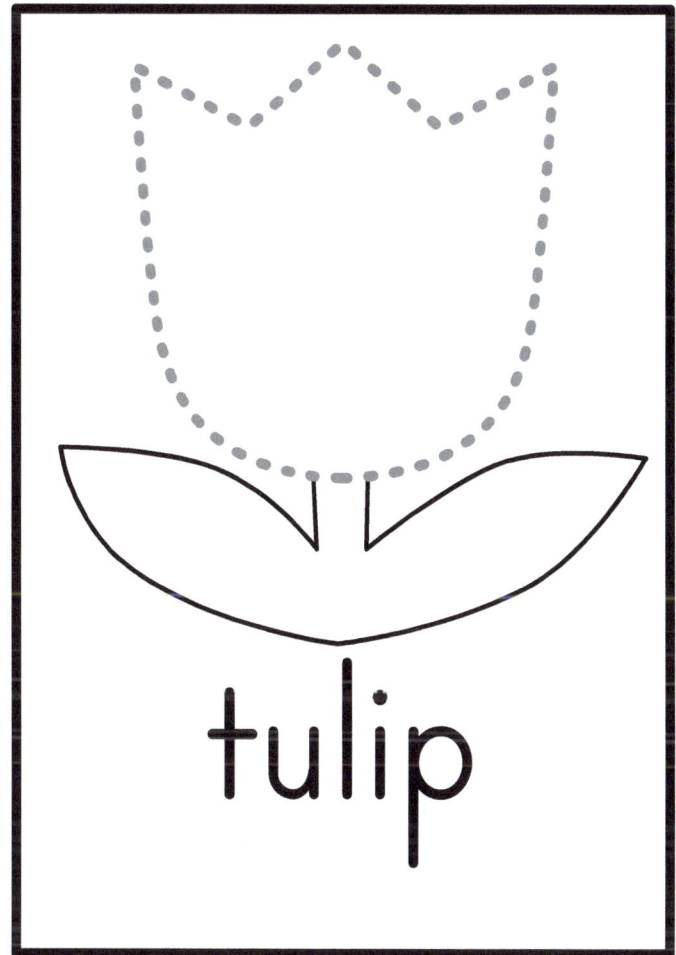

✂ Cut out this card along the bold line. ▶

What You Will Need:

crayons   scissors
paint brush   glue
glitter

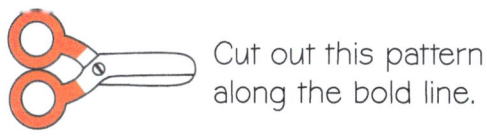

✂ Cut out this pattern along the bold line. ▼

What to Do:

1. Trace the dotted line.
2. Color and cut out the card.
3. Color and cut out the tulip pattern.
4. Glue the tulip cutout on the card.
5. Apply glue with a paint brush, then sprinkle glitter on the tulip.

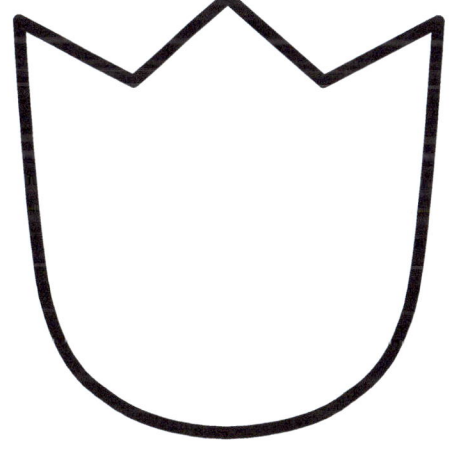

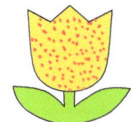 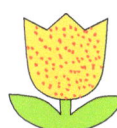 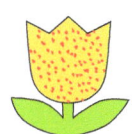 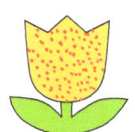 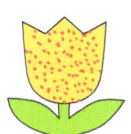 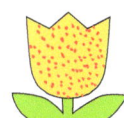 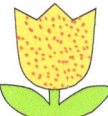 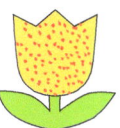 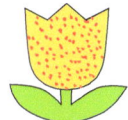

Blank Page

A Cutting Practice Page

Start at the dot and follow each arrow to practice cutting along the dotted lines.

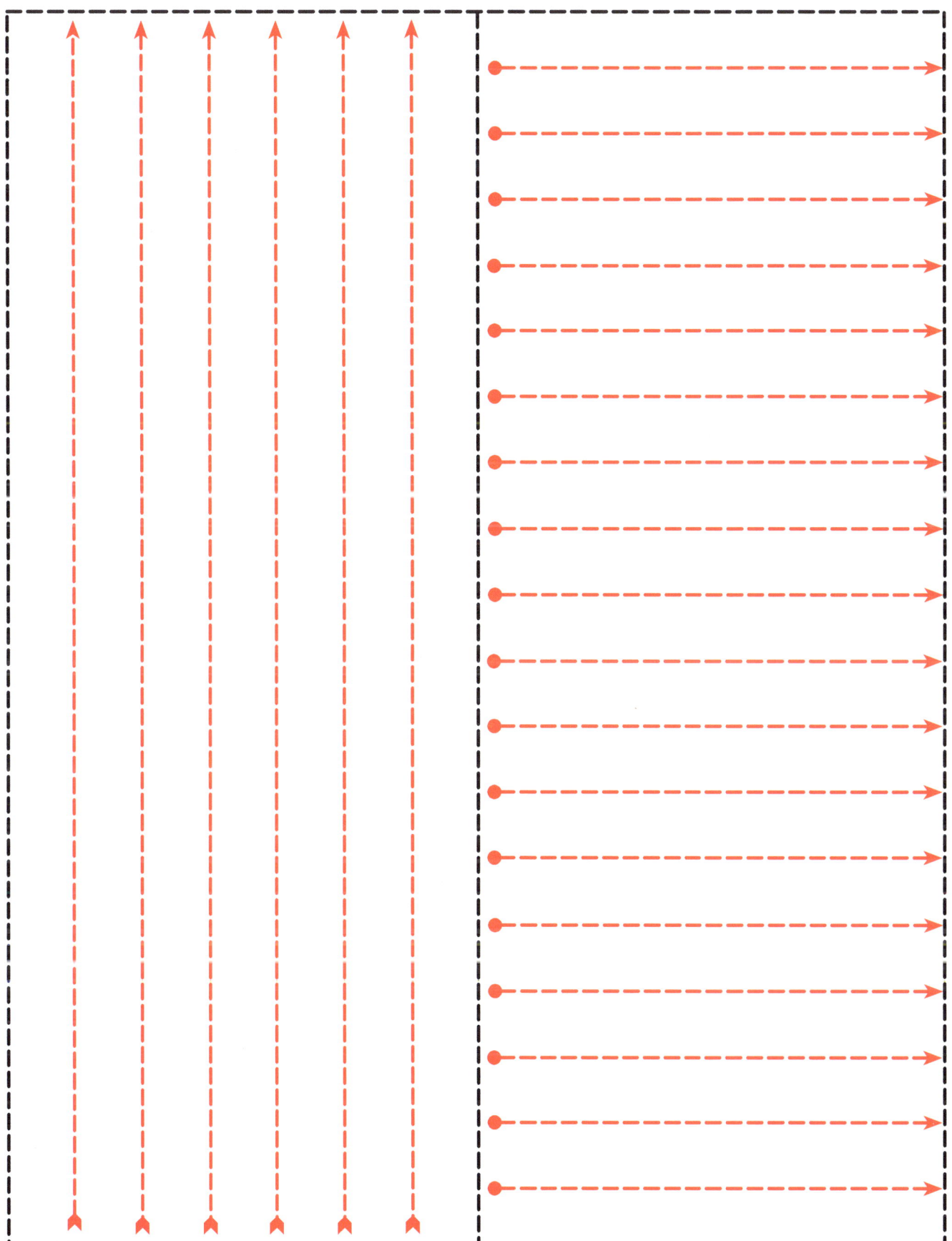

Blank Page

A Cutting Practice Page

Start at the dot and follow each arrow to practice cutting along the dotted lines.

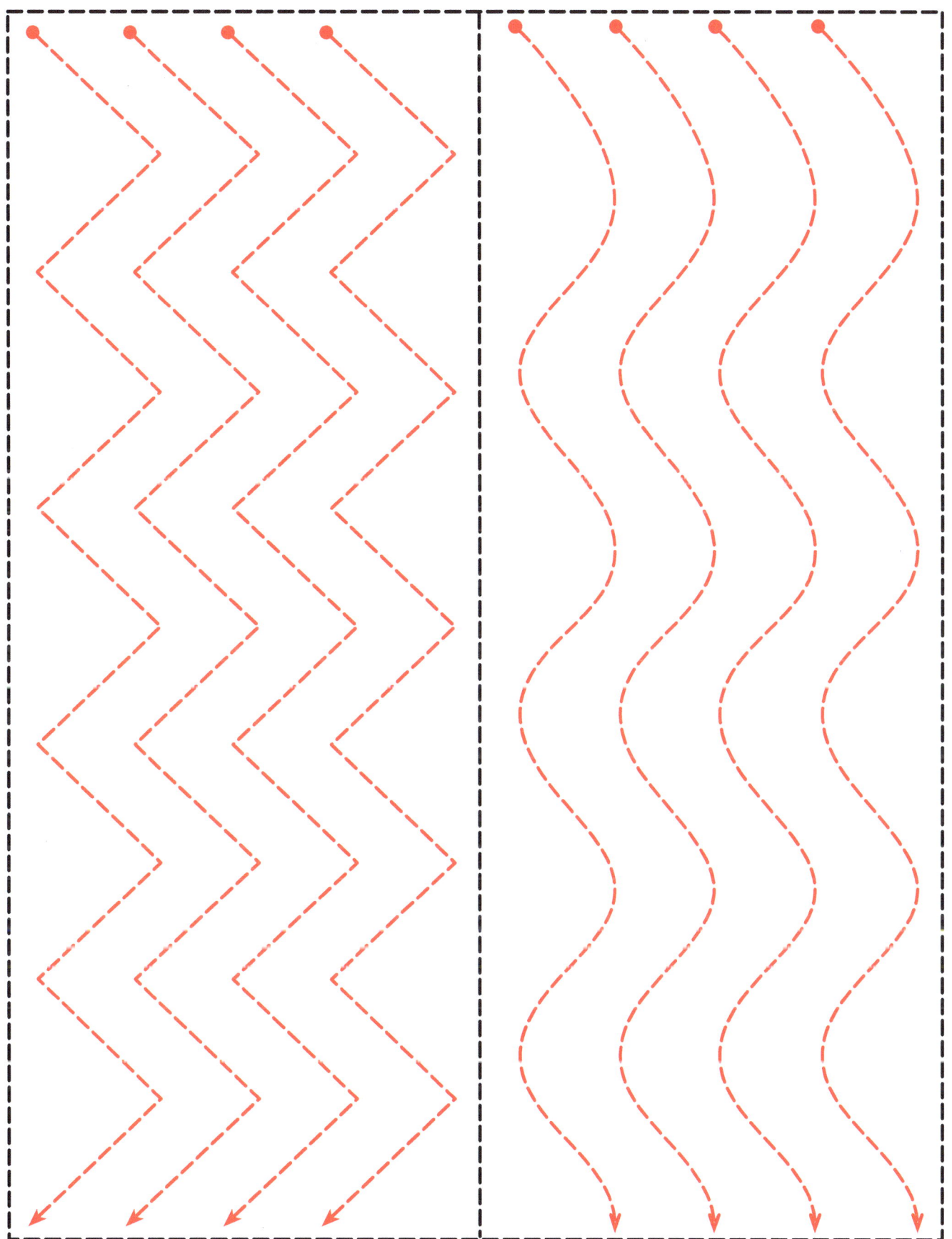

Blank Page